TIME CAPSULE—1944

A Story of World War II

MYRON C. PETERSON

iUniverse, Inc.
Bloomington

Time Capsule—1944
A Story of World War II

iUniverse books may be ordered through booksellers or by contacting:

iUniverse
1663 Liberty Drive
Bloomington, IN 47403
www.iuniverse.com
1-800-Authors (1-800-288-4677)

Because of the dynamic nature of the Internet, any Web addresses or links contained in this book may have changed since publication and may no longer be valid. The views expressed in this work are solely those of the author and do not necessarily reflect the views of the publisher, and the publisher hereby disclaims any responsibility for them.

Any people depicted in stock imagery provided by Thinkstock are models, and such images are being used for illustrative purposes only.

Certain stock imagery © Thinkstock.

ISBN: 978-1-4502-8568-1 (sc)
ISBN: 978-1-4502-8569-8 (ebook)
ISBN: 978-1-4502-8570-4 (dj)

Printed in the United States of America

iUniverse rev. date: 1/19/2011

INTRODUCTION

It is hard for civilized people to imagine what took place in Italy only a short time ago. Armed bands roamed the mountains hunting, attacking and killing each other backed by the most deadly weapons two powerful national states could provide. All the savagery was being explained and applauded with moral justification, for the two countries were at war. The year was nineteen forty-four.

This book is a story of true events that should have been written long ago. Yet, it is a novel because the characters and names are fictitious. It is basically" the story of a few men, part of an infantry squad; for in the highly organized army with its units within units where privacy was non existant, each man was actually alone. With his lifelines thrown out in all directions to family, friends and acquaintances, he eagerly wrote letters trying to keep all lines of communication open. He waited anxiously at mail call.

He was as an alien from another planet thrust into a hostile, foreign environment. Supported by an organized system that pushed him relentlessly forward, he only knew the few people in his immediate squad, or sometimes, when he came to the front as a replacement, he knew no one at all and faced death amid strangers.

Such people as those in the story were very real at the time. However, knowing that time and place cannot be divorced from each other, none of what is written exists anymore. None of the people exist either, for those who are still living are as different as the places where the events took place. This is just a time capsule that I will open briefly, for I was the only witness to many of these actions- As a witness, as well as a participant, I would like to lead you through these pages so you will know the courageous suffering and personal discipline of some of the very young men of my generation who did not want to be soldiers.

We did not want to go to war and our families dreaded it. Many of us had fathers or other relatives who had been in the first world war and we had heard true stories of the brutal fighting. Yet, as is probably always true, we could not imagine what it would really be like.

The young men are sent to war, and they do not want to die. Great causes, emotional nationalism and the determination to settle things by war are the luxuries of those who will not have to pick up the guns and use them.

It was a common saying among combat soldiers that the closer you got to the front the less hatred there was for the enemy. In rear areas and at home patriotism was at a fever pitch. At the front you fought the enemy to stay alive, but you knew that he often was another victim of the war.

This is not to imply that we were unwilling to fight. Our country had been attacked and we knew it must be defended. We were losers in a lottery, but we were not the stereotyped characters of many war stories, tough, swearing sergeants and give 'em hell heroes. We were draftees, your neighbors down the street who had been put in uniform, given a few months of training and sent off to do our duty. That is an old story. This book tells what happened.

THE CAST

Leading Characters:

Marty Staff Sergeant The squad leader
Denny Staff Sergeant Platoon Leader
Ayers Private First Class Rifleman
Martin Sergeant Assistant squad leader
Allen Corporal Platoon Medic
Wallace Private First Class Rifleman
Mathews Captain Company Commander
James Lieutenant Company Officer

Other riflemen: Rule, Scotty, Malik, Truett, Davis, Soroyan, Bradford

And many other extras.

The Witness

Ron Clifford Private First Class Rifleman

I was the witness, as well as a participant in these actions It was not by choice, but according to my destiny. I graduated from high school in June 1943 and was immediately drafted.

After basic training with the tank destroyers in Texas I was transferred to the infantry and went on maneuvers in the mountains of California, but that is another story.

My infantry division was broken up and the enlisted men were sent over seas as replacements. We went on the troopship General Mann to Oran in Africa. After a few weeks we traveled by convoy to Italy and were sent to the replacement depot at Caserta. That, also, is another story.

From there I went to the front as a replacement. This is the story of the combat experiences that followed.

THE LETTERS

The letters linked my mind to the other world and kept my dreams alive. Through them I came to know my family and friends better than ever before. I developed a deeper relationship with my family, especially my father who had never expressed his emotions verbally, but could do it very well in writing.

My father had enlisted in the army during the first world war and had risen to the rank of captain. He did not see combat duty, but was stationed along the Mexican border to prevent the raids by Pancho Villa. He had a favorable view of the army, but did not want me to go to war.

When I was drafted my mother's greatest fear was realized. She had two brothers who had been in the first world war and one of them had been in the heavy fighting in France. He had been gassed and was never well after that.

My older sister, Betty, left home at the same time that I went into the army. She married a service man who was attending college under the Army Specialized Training Program. He was transferred to Illinois and she went there to be with him.

Gladys, my other sister, had graduated from high school a year ahead of me and worked as a bookkeeper. She lived at home during the war.

This was my family, and one of them wrote to me almost every day. There were also letters from close friends. The girls were working or going to school, while most of the boys were in the service.

THE PRELUDE

August 1943

Dear Son,

Have been getting quite a kick out of reading your letters as your experiences are quite similar to my own first days of army life. So keep your chin up. You will survive O.K. but if they serve you mule meat don't bray.

Things here at home are just going along almost as usual. Have been painting your bedroom all ivory and the whole house smells of paint. Have my store teeth and am having a dickens of a time with them but then Mother is having fun too with a new set. Gladys is job hunting again. That government job didn't prove so hot.

Am glad to hear you are qualified for special training as most anything beats combat. Also you would find it pretty nice if you could get a commission or some special position. Do your best son and I don't think you will ever regret it under the circumstances.

I would rather have postponed your education for another year but there was nothing I could do about it. Anyway keep a stiff upper lip and show them you can soldier with the best of them and better than the great majority. And use your head —it may save your arms and feet a lot of work—and if there is anything we can send you or do for you just ask and we will do our best.

With Best Wishes,
Dad

September 1943

Dear Son,

Your letter was the finest birthday present I had ever hoped to receive and I am really proud of you. Mom and I both thank the Lord for a son such as you are and we will keep the home fires burning brightly for your return.

I feared you might be coursened by association with the lower moral standards men so often adopt when thrown together in war and drilled in the unholy art of war and destruction and killing. As you stated I have been through it and knew men at their worst. However, son, if it should come to actual combat for you you will learn that these same men have some very sterling qualities as well as their faults. I have heard from many sources that the modern American army does not have any enthusiasm for this war and I don't blame them, but they are also more serious than we were.

I would like to ask you to go out of your way a bit to get personally acquainted with your chaplain and if you can find time to read your bible perhaps you can find the answers to some of the things you are bound to come in contact with as your training progresses.

Life at home is going on as usual. Two empty places at the table, and we sure miss your talking at dinner. However, Mom and Gladys still carry on, only not as lively as when you put in your bit.

You should see me struggling with my new store teeth. They made a sore in my mouth but I'm gradually getting used to them.

In spite of the fact that this is a financial war I think it is really more than that, but won't try to explain until I see you. Anyway son, when you do come back you will have something to look back on plus something no man who has never worn the uniform can have. As time goes by you will come to understand what I mean by that.

I think a few of the fellows and their wives from the plant are coming over Saturday night to help celebrate my birthday, and we may go out to a dance. Anyway, if they come we are going to have a good time.

Will close now hoping you have the best of luck and gradually harden up so your work won't be so tiring, and again, believe me we are sure proud of you.

Love,
Dad

November 1943

Dear Son,

Today is my day off so I worked all night last night and slept until eleven a,m, today. Your pictures and two letters came today and from your pictures you must be filling out in the face.

About Mother taking shots from the doctor, I want you to know they are for perfectly natural changes for a woman at her age and are merely to help her nervous system and build her up.

Neither of us are worried about a thing. However, we are concerned with your and Betty's absence. You know, after having the house full for so many years and then have you both leave at the same time does make things lonesome. The first day you were away was the hardest. I don't know how Mother made out, but when I came home from work she was awfully quiet. Then we sat down to eat and it was pretty gloomy. I looked at Mother and she burst into tears and so did I. However, that feeling of lonesome-ness wore off and while we miss you very much we know you are all right and will be for a long time or until such a time as they send you over seas. As your training is not over yet, we have no fear of that.

Life goes on here as usual. The cat growls for more horse meat. Gladys and Mother have their spats as usual, but not as often. I come home from the plant and let off steam cussing them and threatening to quit, but never do. There's only one change, Mother and I go out a little more often than we used to and I have one night of bowling.

We have met quite a few people through our legion membership and believe it will build to quite a circle of friendship.

Am glad to hear they are slowing up on your training and you are getting a little more sleep and they're getting more human. You see I know what it is to be so tired that you would give anything for a little rest and something to eat. Before I got my bars I spent all my pay for eats too.

I wanted to erase any worry from your mind about Mother, but probably put it badly. Anyway, we will be waiting for you as healthy as when you left and will welcome you when you come with a display of pep and love that will make your eyes pop out.

Love from Dad

April 1944

Dear Son,

It has been a week without a word from you and as your nineteenth birthday is tomorrow am wondering how you are getting along.

This is the Easter season, and you know Easter is closely connected with you. Nineteen years ago on Good Friday at about eight in the morning you appeared on the scene with a hearty cry and with the exception of the past few months you have filled our home with joy and life.

Mother and Gladys have a small present for you and will mail it as soon as we hear from you again. We haven't heard from Betty since the first and am wondering about her too.

This Easter season has been very windy and the palm trees have lost quite a few of their fronds—almost as good as being pruned. The streets are littered with branches. However, I had to work as usual so didn't mind the wind too much.

I am wondering about Betty's finances. We could help her a bit if she should be short. Feel like giving her a good spanking for not keeping in closer touch. Yes, I know Dad isn't much of a letter writer, but then I have looked after all of your welfare for so many years that the habit kind of sticks and I want ray fingers in it yet. Crude way of putting it but I think you will understand.

Mother got a new suit for Easter and I was supposed to get one too, but haven't had time to go to town and won't for another week. Just now I only get two days off a month and then I usually have to work fifteen or sixteen hours in one day to get it. It's making my paycheck run up to three hundred a month.

Friday I worked to midnight and then had to drive home on the rim as one of my tires let go and my spare is shot. Now I have to fight the O.P.A. as they only grant tires for occupational use. I'm going after them for a larger amount of gasoline too. They have cut us to two gallons weekly and you can't go anyplace on that.

Would like to get a better car, but they want a fortune for cars now, and you can't get gasoline for them. So what's the use.

Will close for now hoping you get enough breaks so you can enjoy a happy birthday. That turkey dinner still goes whenever you can get home long enough to enjoy it and give us time to prepare it.

So, many happy returns of the day and many more of them.

Love from Dad

The Story

Italy in the Summer of 1944

Kill the present with a song
The survivors are the strong
To live longer
Learn how to play the game
Always the same
War is the human play
That's endless.

ONE

"If I were in the infantry again I think I'd be worried about the Gothic Line. It's nice to see you Yanks so happy," Everet, the British sergeant major lifts his glass of cognac. "Then, again, what else can you do? When we were fighting Rommel in the desert it was hot as hell and all we had to eat was bully beef. It was bully beef, bully beef, bully beef! Yet, I think our morale was higher then than it is now."

"We're happy because we're not going to have to worry about that Gothic Line," Ayers says. "Keep the vino flowing. Tonight we feel like celebrating. We've finally been placed in reserve! Our whole damn division has been placed in Fifth Army reserve!"

"That's right," Marty nods. "The Eighty-fifth took over our place in the line. We exchanged places. They've been in reserve since the fall of Rome--over two months. Now it's our turn!"

"Well, this is more of an occasion than I imagined," Everet grins. "When we planned this party we thought we'd cheer you up, but you don't need much of that."

"We're flying high tonight," Ayers agrees. "Look around. Our whole platoon is getting smashed."

"Why not?" Everet nods. "What else can you do in this bloody country?"

The party has been going on for two hours and the empty bottles are mounting. Outside of a little vino it is the first liquor most of us have seen in months.

In fact, most of us aren't even legal drinking age. Of the twelve men in the squad only Marty, the squad leader, and Martin, the assistant, are over twenty-one. Marty is the old man of the group at twenty-three. Martin is twenty-one. The rest, including myself, are all nineteen.

However, in the army age doesn't matter. It's how you do your job that counts. In a combat zone who worries about trivialities?

This friendly and somewhat drunken association of allies that is extending late into the night started in a very casual way.

When our company pulled back from the front the trucks left us in the middle of an olive orchard near Florence during a heavy rain storm. The supply trucks with the tents had failed to meet us.

We stood around all afternoon waiting in the driving rain. It was too muddy to sit down anywhere and we had no field jackets or rain coats. All we could do was shrug up our shoulders to try to keep the cold water that was pouring off our helmets from going down our necks.

There were some farm houses near-by, but we had received orders not to bother the local civilians. For a while most of us sang to keep up morale. We were led by Barnes, a big rifleman from New York who had a booming voice, but gradually the number of singers dwindled until Barnes' voice was all we could hear.

"Where the hell is everyone going?" Ayers asked.

"Anyplace would be better than this," I said.

"Let's check out that house over there," Ayers suggested. "Maybe there's a stable. An American soldier should rate as high as a cow."

I was agreeable to this. With evening coming on and still no sign of the trucks with the tents, it seemed ridiculous to stand around in the dark.

As we suspected, a room on the back of the house turned out to be a stable, and we weren't surprised to find most of our platoon lying in the hay.

"Go into the house," Martin said when he saw us dripping water all over. "There's a fire in the fireplace and the people will let you dry off. Go on! Everyone's been doing it."

We followed the suggestion and the farmer's wife pushed us over to the roaring fire. When we were dry we joined the rest of our buddies in the soft hay. The next morning the weather cleared and the supplies arrived. We were busy setting up the camp when the English sergeant major wandered into the area and introduced himself.

"Everet's the name," he said smiling. "I'm with that signal company just down the road. We saw you arrive yesterday during that beastly storm, so I thought I'd drop over and invite a few of you Yanks to a party we're having tonight."

"We never turn down an invitation to a party," Ayers said, and there was a chorus of agreement from all around.

"Don't worry about the drinks," Everet said. "We've plenty of cognac and vermouth on hand. Every day we send someone out for a fresh supply."

Once the party started all formality melted away and shyness faded. The British and Americans mingled together like cousins at a family reunion, and the abundance of vermouth killed any inhibitions.

"This place is like a canteen," I tell Everet as I look around at the large room that opens to a walled courtyard. It easily accommodates the hundred or more men who are standing around or sitting at the picnic style tables.

"We selected the place for that reason," Everet agrees.

The party is well planned and includes entertainment. Some of the British hosts are dressed up in funny clothes and begin acting out comedy skits and telling dirty jokes. When there is a lull, small groups get up to sing. The British start it and then urge the Americans to follow suite.

When a song is familiar, others standing around the room join in the singing. Some are songs that only the British know, and there are others that only the Americans know, but there are a surprising number that everyone sings together.

"I'm Clemens," an English soldier extends his hand to me. "And this is Jock," he adds, placing his hand on a buddy's shoulder. "We call him Jock because he's from Wales. Everyone from Wales is Jock."

"Like someone from Texas is Tex," I suggest.

"That's it," Clemens smiles.

"Well, I'm Ron ," I introduce myself. "I'm from California."

"California! Hollywood!" Clemens exclaims.

"From Los Angeles—Hollywood is part of Los Angeles."

"American pictures are great. Do you ever see any of the movie stars?"

"I've seen a few—not many."

"I hope you've never seen a British film," Everet joins in, frowning. "They're terrible. The Americans know how to make films."

"Except when they show British royalty," Jock interrupts. "When they show everyone bowing down and all I just scoot down in my seat."

"Oh, have you met Ayers?" I change the subject. "This is my buddy Ayers."

Ayers smiles showing his very white teeth that are in strong contrast with his olive complexion.

"Ayers and I have been digging in and pitching tent together since I first met him when I joined the company as a replacement."

Ayers has a lean, serious face with dark, alert eyes that dart around, missing very little. He is very social and quick to join into a conversation.

Clemens and Ayers are soon talking on and on. I take another drink of vermouth and let my mind drift back in time. Ayers didn't have that happy look on his face when I first met him. That was the day I first smelled death.

"Every time you go up to the front you get more scared, Wallace said.

Wallace, with his freckled face and boyish smile was sitting on the ground in the middle of the dusty path. His wool, olive drab shirt and pants were already comouflaged by a layer of summer dust. Wallace was talking like a veteran, and although he was only nineteen, to us he was a veteran. He had been at the front for several months as a combat rifleman, and now he was leading our group of twelve men up to his battalion, up to the front.

I still couldn't believe we were getting close, for the countryside looked the same as in the rear areas, the same rolling hills covered with grape vines and stalks of corn. The beautiful summer day was enough to give you spring fever, with fresh green shrubbery all around and a bright blue sky overhead.

"Come on, everyone, the break's over," Wallace said. "And when we start moving, keep down. There could be Jerries in those hills."

We continued our journey that had started at the replacement depot at Caserta a few days before. Trucks hauled us from there to Naples, and in the late afternoon we boarded some waiting ships, infantry landing craft.

After dark our group of flat bottomed boats sailed out of Naples' huge harbor and headed North along the coast. The sea was rough and all night the boats bucked and rolled. They reared high, crashed back and smacked the surface, sending gallons of salt water down below the deck into the large room where we lay on our cramped bunks. Our field packs and rifles were hung on pegs along the walls, but as the small craft shuddered and groaned it smashed our gear to the floor and kept us busy all night picking things up. Who could sleep any way? We were all dazed, light headed and nauseated. I kept stuffing my stomach with crackers hoping to keep everything down.

In the early morning the sea was calm so we were allowed up on deck. Weak in the knees, we lined the rail to watch as we entered a small harbor, littered with sunken ships and floating debris. Out in the bay a freighter was anchored, her hoists discharging cargo into an amphibious landing craft tied along side.

Our little ship pulled neatly up to a shattered dock and efficiently dropped a side ramp. When the ship's engines stopped, the sudden, absolute silence was startling.

We eagerly disembarked, throwing our packs down on the dock to create our own seats, and soon everyone was sprawled around waiting for the trucks that were scheduled to meet us.

We passed the time watching the amphibious craft, called a duck, pull away from the freighter in the bay and plow through the blue water to the shore, where, like a giant turtle, it lumbered up onto the sand. It seemed like a slow, unpressured operation with only three men working on the gigantic task of unloading supplies.

The tranquility of the morning was shattered by high pitched squeeling and the roaring of engines as a column of trucks filled the air with dust. Soon we were aboard and moving again.

When we left the dock area and entered the town a spontaneous hush fell over us. We were bouncing along over pieces of rock as the trucks picked their way through a labyrinth of devastation. The total destruction had left the town a jungle of rubble. We moved along passing block after block where the buildings were reduced to piles of rock a few feet high. In the entire town only a few tottering piles of rubble broke the skyline.

The church, the heart of this small town's life, was marked by a pile of scattered stone and the broken wall of the sanctuary. A woman, an old man and two children were picking among the ruins gathering sacred objects.

Beside the town sprawled the cause of its destruction, the large mass of twisted iron beams and wrecked railroad cars that had once been a steel mill. Allied bombers had left it black and broken. A boxcar and a locomotive were sticking out of a mountain side above the town at grotesque angles as if they were gathered by a giant hand and hurled in rage.

An older soldier sitting next to me in the truck watched for a while and then spoke angrily.

"If there was a God in heaven do you think he would permit this?"

I said nothing, but looked in stunned silence at this massive ruin. There was little left of this historic town of Piombino.

The persistant trucks carried us away from the depressing scene and into the green hills of the countryside. We passed through small villages filled with cheering people holding up their hands, waving and giving us the V sign. And there were children calling out for candy, which the G.I.s took from their rations and tossed from the trucks. The adults also waited with anxious faces, hoping for cigarettes.

We passed through the courtyard of a convent and onto an open valley where army engineers were constructing a new camp. There were great piles of equipment in the fields, pieces of a jig saw puzzle waiting to be assembled. As yet there was no water, but a portable derrick marked the place where the engineers were drilling a-well. At this point our trucks stopped to wait for darkness before continuing the journey.

Some of the waiting G.I.s went into the surrounding fields and spent the time helping the local farmers pitch hay into a brightly colored cart. The farmers laughed and thanked everyone. They said they were short handed because of the war. Then they asked if it were true that the American farmers had machines to do all the work. Communication was difficult because of our limited knowledge of the language, but somehow there was understanding.

More trucks arrived and two G.I.s began tossing duffle bags off the trucks into the fields. When they yelled for us to find our own we began searching through the mounds. The bags were all alike except for the black stenciled names on them. After combing through them all several times I was convinced that my bag wasn't there.

"Where are the rest?" I asked the driver. "That's it," he said. "There are no more." "But, mine is missing," I protested.

"These are all we have," he said. "Maybe it got sent to the wrong place. It'll catch up with you later."

With the coming of night the line of metal machines started forward again. Like nocturnal animals they crawled through the moonless night without headlights, creeping along roads that I couldn't see. How could our silent driver find his way through the hilly terrain?

When a wrecked truck blocked the road, we were ordered out and told to bed down for the night. Earlier we had heard some artillery firing in the distance, but it had become as completely silent as it was dark.

In the morning the trucks tried to take us farther, but when we entered a small village we encountered another problem. A burned out jeep stretched its black skeletin across our path. Just as the drivers got out to investigate, some enemy artillery shells blasted the town. Instinctively, abandoning the trucks we all raced for cover.

Mortar shells were falling in a ravine ahead of us, so we were ordered to wait until the afternoon before attempting to move forward. Later, when we finally started out again, another mortar barrage hit the ravine. We were then told to dig slit trenches and prepare to spend the night.

Just before sundown we saw some G.I.s taking some German prisoners to the rear. The Jerries stumbled along single file with their hands resting on the tops of their heads.

During the night we heard the truck engines start up again. Dark shadows backed up and pulled away, deserting us, going like phantoms in the night back along the invisible road. Overhead we heard the hiss of passing artillery shells.

At the first light of morning a young lieutenant called out our names and assigned us to company groups. From that point on we would proceed on foot.

Wallace had been sent back to lead our twelve man group of replacements up to our companies. We had been following him for six hours along a narrow dusty path. The weather was hot and our canteens had been almost dry for hours. Wallace told us that rain water puddles was about the only source of water around.

"We're leaving the path now," Wallace said. "We're almost there."

Climbing up a small hill we walked into a forest of large trees with massive, spreading limbs. The shadowy patches on the ground created moving patterns with the sunlight, but suddenly those shadows were helmets and faces. We were walking among clusters of men reclining on the ground or sitting with their backs propped up against the trees. Most of them were quietly eating their K rations.

"This is your company," Wallace said, turning to me. "You're in the same company I'm in. Over there is Denny, your platoon sergeant."

Sergeant Denny was sitting casually on the ground leaning against a tree. He was small with a trim, muscular build. His blue eyes were sparkling and friendly, and his close cut red hair matched his short mustache. He smiled, without getting up, when Wallace introduced me.

"You'll be in the first platoon," he said without hesitation. "Is that a communication unit?" I asked. "I'm a telephone lineman."

"We don't need any lineman," Denny abruptly answered. "Here you're a rifleman."

"But I've never been trained as a rifleman," I protested. "I was in the tank destroyers in basic, and have been in communications section of a headquarters company since then."

"Maybe sometime we'll need a lineman," Denny said. "Now we need riflemen, so you're a rifleman."

It was settled, and I was not happy about this turn of events. I had never been in a line company and was not sure what was expected of me.

"Where's the front?" I asked.

"This is it," Denny answered.

"But it's so quiet. I don't hear any shooting."

"It wasn't quiet a short while ago," Denny said. "We caught the Krauts trying to pull back. There's a dead one over there."

He gestered with his head, and then added, "But sit down and have a ration. It's time to eat."

Denny smiled as he tossed the box to me. I thanked him and suddenly felt hungry.

As I walked around looking for a place to sit down I found I was near the body of the dead German. I had not seen a dead soldier before and the image was burned into my memory.

He was sprawled partly in a slit trench and partly out. His head was thrown back and flies were crawling around his open mouth and across his open blue eyes.

"He was a sniper," Denny said. "We surprised him from behind."

His skin was a strange yellow color. A wallet, identification papers and cards were scattered on the ground. He had been carving his name on the tree branch that he had placed across his slit trench for camouflage. He was half finished when he was shot.

I picked up the card and looked at it, studying the picture of the handsome, smiling face. He had been in the German army since nineteen forty. He had fought in Russia.

Down the hill in a field of weeds were some wrecked German trucks. For the first time I saw the black cross insignia.

Denny had been watching me all the time.

"They tried to bring up some trucks to evacuate their men," he said, "but we hit them."

"Aren't we going to bury him?" I asked.

"You can if you want to, but you'll get mighty tired if you try to bury every dead Jerry."

Turning from the body I sat down to eat my rations, but I was down wind from the body and it was starting to smell. I tasted the can of cheese and took a bite of the biscuit, but I had no appetite. The smell of the body and the smell of the cheese had somehow become linked in my memory.

In the first platoon I was assigned to the first squad. My squad leader, Sergeant Martin, stood with his helmet in his hand exposing his blond hair that was cut short like the bristles of a hair brush. Although he was of average height, he was husky and well built like a football player. He was tan, as were all these men who had been living outdoors in the Italian sun. I noticed a slight scar running across his cheek.

"Call me Marty," he said informally. "We have another Sergeant Martin in this squad, so he's Martin and I'm Marty. But I'm a staff sergeant, so I'm one up **on** him."

"You'll need a buddy to dig in with," he added. "It's easier in two's. If you want to you can team up with Ayers."

Ayers came over when he heard his name.

"I don't have anyone to dig in with," he said.

When I nodded he smiled and offered me his hand.

The first thing Ayers did was try to impress me with the idea that all that serenity out there was deceptive.

"There are Krauts all over, and you have to watch out for the snipers. There's been all hell happening around here."

Ayers also took me around and introduced me to the other men in the squad, Malik, Truett, Scotty, Davis and the others.

It was early evening, when the shadows were blurring the landscape that we received orders to move forward., and I soon learned of some of the dangers Ayers was talking about.

With our twelve man squad in the lead, the thirty man platoon left the cover of the trees and started along the dusty trail, walking single file. I was not afraid. I was not nervous. I was nothing but alert. I was aware that I knew nothing of this strange world where destiny had placed me.

Following Ayers, I was keeping an eye on everything he did, but I was also watching Marty. Ayers had told me that Marty had six months of combat experience and had never been wounded. It was my personal strategy to do whatever Marty did until I learned how to survive.

Without warning, just before dark, we were engulfed with shrieking, booming sounds. Flashing light and flying dirt was all around us.

Everyone dropped to the ground and I lay trembling with my face in the dust.

Within a few minutes the rumbling stopped as abruptly as it had started. Again there was silence. With some hesitation the men got to their feet, arranged their light packs and adjusted the gas masks that hung from their shoulders. The line began to move forward again.

Ayers looked back at me, and he was the only one to speak.

"That was nothing!"

We continued walking along the path until it was so dark that I couldn't see anything except the moving shadow ahead of me that I knew was Ayer's back. Finally the order came to stop and dig in.

Using the small pick that I carried on my belt I started to dig along the trail. Ayers had a shovel, and soon we had a hole about six feet long and three feet deep.

"We could dig faster if you'd get a shovel," Ayers said.

"I've always liked a pick," I said. "You can get the rocks out. I used one all through maneuvers in California."

"This is the new type," Ayers continued, ignoring my protest. "You can adjust the blade to make it like a pick, or you can make it straight like a shovel. When somebody gets hit you can pick one up."

We climbed into our crude bed and stretched out. Since the trench wasn't very wide we were pressed together, but I was tired and fell asleep quickly. My helmet was a bulky pillow, but I kept it on.

Two

A replacement is the most likely to become a casualty because he isn't wise to the dangers and is likely to take too many chances. Those words from basic training should have haunted me as I prepared for my first day of action at the front. Before the day was over I remembered them much better.

"Prepare to move out. Prepare to move out. Prepare to move out," the words passed from mouth to mouth.

The summer sky was still dark when we left the high country and walked down among the dense grapes and corn fields that covered the rolling hills in the valley floor. With the tall corn stalks all around us it was difficult to see more than a few yards in any directions.

"A and B companies will lead the assault," Denny explained. "We'll follow in reserve to give assistance where it's needed."

We could see a white farm house on the highest hill in the valley, and that was the objective.

"The Krauts are entrenched all around it," Denny said.

"They could be anywhere in these corn fields," Ayers added.

We continued through the valley walking single file until we reached the base of the hill. There, in a dry stream bed, we stopped and dug our slit trenches. Digging in the sandy soil was easy and soon Ayers and I had a deep hole.

We were out in the open with no shade around us and the sun was rising high into a cloudless sky. As the time slowly passed, the heat became more and more oppressive.

I looked down the row of men sitting in the slit trenches and it reminded me of an old tin type photograph. Everyone was sitting frozen in his dusty hole staring blankly at the walls of green around him. The only movement was the heat waves rising froin the dark helmets. It seemed there was nothing to do but be patient and wait, but that wasn't my style. My muscles were tense and my mind restless.

Dug in along side of us were Marty and Martin. On the other side were Malik and Davis and next to them were Scotty and Truett.

"Where are the guys in the squad from?" I asked Ayers. "Where's Marty from?"

"Marty's from Pennsylvania, like me. I don't know where Scotty's from, but it's down South—you can tell by the accent. Truett's from New England somewhere. He's French. Scotty and Truett are buddy buddy--do everything together."

"What about Malik? He seemed cheerful and friendly yesterday, but today he's not talking to anyone."

"Malik's a Pole-from somewhere in the East. He's a good guy, but he worries alot. He's been getting more depressed all the time."

Everything lapsed into silence again as I studied Marty and Martin. Neither of them were moving or talking. I wondered about their attitude toward replacements. I was taking someone's place, someone who had been a casualty. I wondered if he had been a good buddy to them. I could see where a squad was like a family. The men lived together night and day with each person depending on the others to do their parts to insure survival in this deadly game. I came into this world as a total stranger and felt a little like an intruder. I had to get to know everyone, and it was possible the others didn't want to know me too well. It would hurt less if a stranger became a casualty.

The sun was growing hotter and I had a fierce thirst. The last drop of water had been drained from my two canteens. I had been hoarding it and rationing myself for the past two days, remembering that on my way to the front I hadn't passed a well or seen a water hole, and Ayers said there had been no cans of water coming up with the supplies. When we entered the valley I picked some grapes and sucked on them to kill my thirst, but where we were dug in there were only corn fields. Ayers reminded me that I was not alone in my suffering. Everyone was out of water.

By mid day the sun was scorching. Our wool shirts were sticking to our sweaty bodies, and nothing seemed to be happening at all. Where were A and B companies? We hadn't heard any shooting. If we could capture the house on the hill we would gain control of the well.

As I studied the fields around us, I felt certain there was another source of water close by. At the far end of the corn field, not fifty yards away, I could see a mass of green reeds. It seemed likely there was a pond or stream over there. What a temptation it was!

"This is a hell of a spot," Ayers said. "Look at this hill. It's a perfect place for observation. The Jerries have a view of the whole valley."

I was hardly listening, for I had come to a decision.

"I'll go after water if someone will go with me," I said.

The only response to my voluntary suggestion was silence.

"The sun must be affecting your brain," Ayers said.

We all sat silently in the sun for a while longer and then from down the line a voice spoke up.

"If you still want to go for water, I'll go with you."

"I will too," another said.

The two volunteers were not from my squad, but they were in my platoon. I didn't know either of them. Instinctively they stayed low to the ground as they crawled over to my slit trench. Still crawling, the three of us started across the open, sandy ground that lay between our trenches and the corn field.

"Crack!" a bullet kicked up the dirt beside me.

Spinning around, I lunged and dived back into the slit trench.

"Are you hit?" Marty asked.

"No," I answered, "but I think we'd better go a different way. "

Ayers must have been right when he said the sun had affected my brain, because I was still determined to get the water. My two new buddies were still willing to go with me. A week later, with more combat experience, I wouldn't have considered trying it.

Without hesitation we crawled down the row of slit trenches and from a new spot started out again to cross the open ground. Sliding on our stomachs we pulled our bodies toward the rows of corn. This time there were no shots.

Among the corn, we each crawled rapidly down a different row, trying not to stir up any dust or touch anything that could move. Soon the dirt beneath our hands turned to mud and the stalks were replaced by reeds. We were within easy reach of the cool water.

When I saw the pond with the moist, green lilly pads floating on its surface, I touched my feverish face to the water, absorbing its coolness. Taking off my helmet, I soaked my entire head before taking time to fill the canteens. I dipped the helmet into the intoxicating liquid, wanting to take back as much of it as possible.

The refreshing moisture of the shaded pond was inviting me to stay, but when I saw the anxious looks on my buddies' faces, I quickly turned around.

"Let's get the hell back," one of them said.

It was hard to crawl without spilling the water as I pushed the full helmet ahead of me. I also had to watch my elbows, for the corn stalks were close together forming a very narrow row. My progress was so slow that I began to feel anxious, and as I approached the slit trenches I worried about crossing those last few yards in the open. Could I make it moving like a turtle?

When I finally reached the edge of the cornfield speed and surprise seemed the best strategy. Rising to my knees, I raced across the sand, handing the helmet to Ayer's outstretched hands as I leaped and tumbled into the trench.

The helmet was passed around to everyone in the squad and each man touched it to his lips to take a deep drink.

As they drank the ground quivered and rumbled. The air was filled with green reeds and flying dirt. In an instant the Krauts had destroyed the pond with a mortar barrage. The attack was brief, and when the dust settled all signs of the cool water had vanished.

"From that hill they can see everything," Ayers said.

"I'm just glad my buddies were anxious to get back," I said.

Down the line of trenches there was a small fruit tree that provided the only shade around. Denny and another G.I. had climbed out of their hole and were sitting back under the thin branches resting against the trunk.

"Crack!" A rifle shot! Denny was the lucky one. The man beside him was hit between the eyes and fell over dead.

Where was the sniper? We could see nothing but corn stalks and grape vines all over the hill. Was the Kraut close or up on the top of the hill using a telescopic sight?

"God, Denny's lucky!" Ayers said. "A while back the Krauts fired an airburst and it killed the guys on both sides of him and he was untouched."

"It'll be getting dark soon and the Krauts will be coming after us," Marty said. "They know we're here and they could be closing in right now, just waiting."

"I'd like to know what's going on," Ayers said. "The bastards that got us into this better get us out."

Ayers words were quickly answered as Denny came crawling down the line whispering to everyone.

"As soon as it gets dark we'll move out, but there can't be any noise. The Krauts are close, and if they hear us they'll attack."

"Watch the metal equipment," Marty cautioned. "Watch the canteens and tools. Don't let anything hit together."

We had a lot of metal: helmets, canteens, grenades, bandoliers of ammunition, rifles, shovels. An accident, or one careless man could bring swift destruction to everyone.

It was dusk when the signal was given to move. Without a sound the entire platoon stepped out of the trenches. It was like in a dream. Everyone was moving together and I couldn't even hear a footstep. There was no sound to give us away, yet, all hell broke loose!

Somewhere very close there was an unseen observer, for we had gone but a few yards away from the trenches when the entire valley boomed to life. Deadly plumes of dirt flew into the air as screaming mortars rained from the sky.

With near panic everyone leaped and dived for any cover he could find. The first thing I saw was a small irrigation ditch that cut through the field, and I sprawled into it. On my way down I fell on top of another man. My rifle caught crosswise across the top of the ditch so that I draped over it.

The Germans were so close that I could hear the clicking sounds as the shells were dropped into the barrels of the mortars. I was splattered with something! Grapes? Or what? Acrid smoke obliterated everything.

Suddenly the shelling stopped. Marty jumped up and started to run. Instantly I raced after him. A swarm of men were running with us, hurtling objects, heading out of the valley and into the hills.

"I'm right behind you," I yelled to Marty. "What do we do now?"

"They'll wipe the valley out with another barrage," he said.

When we reached the tree covered hills we stopped to wait for everyone to assemble. As Marty predicted, the entire valley exploded like an erupting volcano as the Krauts laid down another heavy barrage. We stood looking at a dust bowl.

While we watched the total destruction some of the men laughed and joked. I smiled too, feeling a release of tension. I was still alive and untouched.

We remained on the hill and dug in for the night. Shortly after we finished the slit trenches we saw a jeep creeping slowly through the trees.

"After today we thought everyone could use a hot meal," a voice said.

I couldn't believe it was possible! The cooks had brought our mess kits and two containers of hot food. We sat around in the dark enjoying the hot stew.

That night I lay in the slit trench studying the stars, looking for familiar constellations. They made me feel closer to home. Although it was noon in California I thought maybe my family and friends would soon be looking at those same stars.

I wondered why there had been a pause in the mortar barrage so we were able to get out of the valley. Perhaps it was because of all the dust. The Krauts may have wanted to let the dust settle so they could see the damage and know where to fire the next salvo.

I felt mighty lucky and was amazed that no one in our squad had been hit.

THREE

We were the point, leading the attack. It was our squad's turn. Wary and nervous, I kept my eyes on Marty.

Running single file through the hills we came to a small village that appeared to be deserted. With our hearts in our mouths we raced from building to building, dropping behind any cover, searching constantly with our eyes. There was no one to be seen. The civilians had fled and the Krauts had chosen not to make a stand there.

Beyond the village was our main objective, another farm house on top of a hill. As we started up the trail a German machine gun opened fire and several men in the platoon caught bullets in their packs.

Spreading out, we advanced cautiously, studying the terrain ahead. The orchards and fields were still confusing to me and I couldn't see any sign of the enemy.

We moved on up the hill and everything remained quiet. Soon we could see the house, but it was partly hidden by the trees in the orchard. As we crept closer we could see that it was in the middle of a wide, bare clearing. We would have to cross forty yards of open yard to reach it.

Lieutenant James motioned for the company to spread out along the edge of the orchard and he placed an automatic rifle team so it could fire across the yard and cover the approaches to the house.

There was no sign of any enemy activity, but a German half-track with a fifty caliber machine gun mounted on it was parked near the front door.

Suddenly a G.I. was racing across the clearing toward the house.

"What the hell is he doing?" Denny asked.

We all watched without understanding what was happening, but expecting some Krauts to open fire from the house at any second. It was like watching a Hollywood movie. The G.I. reached the half-track and jumped into the back. Spinning the machine gun toward the house, he fired two short bursts and called for the Germans to come out.

Immediately the door opened and twelve Germans came out with their hands on their heads.

The rest of our company ran across the field and surrounded the prisoners. As I passed the half-track I noticed that the machine gun was a captured American weapon.

One of the Germans who spoke English said the half-track was there to take them back. They were ready to pull out.

For the first time I was standing next to the enemy. Before they had been faceless killers firing at us from hidden positions These Krauts were young kids, and when I saw the white faces and frightened eyes I felt pity. It was my nature to have sympathy for the helpless, and it was hard to hate a scared kid.

"They're lucky," Denny said, reading my thoughts. "The war's over for them."

"The bastards are Krauts," Ayers said. "They kill your buddies and then surrender, expecting to be treated good."

A guard detail marched the twelve prisoners to the rear and we continued our advance until it was dark. We came to another abandoned house and while our officers went inside to check their maps by candle light, we dug our slit trenches in the yard. It was almost midnight before Ayers and I had finished.

It was a hot night so I lay down beside the trench rather than in it. The stars looked close enough to touch.

Like a hushed lullaby the wind sounds of the artillery shells whispered as they passed high overhead. I listened and thought of the madness the Krauts were suffering where the shells were landing.

"Why do you think that guy raced out to that half-track all by himself?" I asked Ayers.

"He was crazyi Read too many war stories," Ayers snorted.

"He was damn lucky," I added. "Any of those Krauts in the house could have winged him."

I should have been tired, but I wasn't sleepy. The word had just come down that we'd be making a dawn attack on a fortified town.

FOUR

The dust made our eyebrows white and the hot sun sent the sweat running down our faces carrying the salty mud into our mouths. This made our thirst worse, and there was no water. Our canteens were empty and there was no anticipation of filling them. The wells at all the farms were dry.

Along the road the dust was ankle deep and the hot July wind sifted it through the grape vines and corn stalks. Our uniforms were camouflaged with it. We tried not to think of cool streams and drinking fountains when all we could see were dry roads and scorched fields.

"There it is," Ayers said.

Our objective had come into view at the top of the next hill. Like a crown on a pointed head, the cluster of buildings huddled together defensively behind the solid walls that met the steep hill on all sides.

"That town looks more like a fort," Martin said.

"All these hill towns are like that," Denny said. "They were built for defense."

"Like everything else in this country," Ayers agreed.

The intimidating walls looked massive and impregnable as they towered above us, and we knew the Krauts were on the other side.

As we neared the base of the hill a sharp "crack" split the morning air.

A sniper! Where was he? The steep slopes of the hill covered with dense shrubbery offered no clues. I could feel myself in the sights of his gun so I left the road to walk among the grape vines.

Everyone else quickly abandoned the road and the entire platoon was spread out. In squad formations we began the steep climb, walking through an orchard. We heard a German machine gun up ahead, its rapid fire answered by a slower American automatic rifle. Our advanced platoon was engaged in a fire fight.

Denny motioned for us to move up to add support. Grabbing a handful of sour grapes, I stuffed them into my mouth to kill the thirst.

"This damn country," Ayers said. "Who wants it? No water, no nothing!"

As we continued to climb, firing our rifles, the Krauts fired back, but slowly withdrew into the security of the town. A number of men in the advanced platoon were hit.

"It could be the damn Italians firing," Ayers said. "Who'd know? The bastards are probably hoping we'll die so they can get back to their German buddies."

Since the Germans had retreated into the town our company assembled in the orchard to plan the attack.

Hey!" a voice rang out. "Here's a wine cellar."

A cave had been dug into the side of the hill and stocked with dozens of bottles of cool red wine. We were jubilant! The bottles quickly passed from hand to hand. There was plenty— enough for the whole squad, the platoon, the company!

"My prayers have been answered," Wallace said.

"Dego red! Aged too!" Truett shouted.

It was an ecstacy of relief to feel the cool liquid drain down my throat. The pleasure of the moment was supreme. It was hard to stop drinking even though I knew it was wine and it was important to keep my head clear. I looked at the bottle and it was half gone. Quickly I handed it to Truett. He had one already, but he took it gladly.

The only way into the town was along the road that led through an open gateway. The walls were built so a heavy gate could bar the way, but a gate was no longer there. The only barrier was the Kraut bullets.

Our strategy was historic and simple. While most of the men concentrated their fire on the opening, a few teams would race into the town and try to get into the closest buildings. We were all gamblers hoping for some luck.

The attack began and the first men disappeared through the gate. We heard firing in the town, so more men raced ahead. I followed Marty and Martin, while Ayers came behind me.

Bullets were nicking the buildings and ricocheting off the cobblestone street. Running and zig-zagging I leaped into the first open doorway. Martin and Ayers jumped in with me.

We were in a small room with a brick floor, and in the middle of the room was someone else.

Seated on a stool, with a large iron kettle in front of her, was a very old Italian woman. With a smile, and without saying anything, she handed me a dipper of cool water.

While the bullets danced around the doorway I touched the dipper to my lips and took a long, cool drink.

"Gracie," I murmured as I handed back the dipper,, and she nodded.

Again she filled the dipper and handed it to Ayers. As each G.I. jumped into the room she handed him a dipper of water.

We continued running from door to door, shooting at all the doors and windows. Bullets ricocheted down the street, but we could not see the enemy. The Krauts were abandoning the buildings before we got to them, and finally, in the late afternoon we saw them leaving the town and retreating down the northern slope.

We followed them out of the town and continued the chase, firing until it was too dark to see anything.

When we dug in for the night we were too tired to talk, but as I shoveled out the dirt I thought of that brave Italian woman who stayed behind to help us. She was the only civilian we saw in the town. In my mind I saw that kind old face and the dipper of cool water.

The next farmhouse was ravaged by the war with evidence of the recent fighting all around. The adobe walls were blackened and scarred from shrapnel and bullets, but the most obvious remnant was a dead Kraut lying face down in the yard near the front door. On his back were all the trappings of a German soldier. He was burdened with a full field pack and even a small metal stove to heat his rations. His canteen and gas mask were still neatly in place. He must have been trying to get away with all his gear when he was hit.

We were no longer concerned with the sight of another dead body, so Marty, Ayers and the rest of the squad walked past it and entered the house.

Men from our company were already inside, but we didn't know them. They were busy doing things that rational soldiers didn't do. They were cleaning up the room, throwing out the debris and straightening up the shattered house.

Noticing our stares, one of them said, "We're going to be staying here for a day or two. We just got the word."

That never happens, I thought, but maybe this time they will be right. We believe what we want to believe.

In the farm yard, near the dead Kraut, there was a well, so I went to check it out, hoping that for once I would find one that wasn't dry.

I turned the crank until the bucket went down very deep. Suddenly it splashed into some water. The Italians would not drink this water, preferring to live on wine; but we had no choice! Although it was madness to take such chances, everyone filled his canteen. It might have been alright if we had had chlorine tablets but whenever I asked Denny for some he said there were none. No one had chlorine tablets.

Since the army couldn't supply us with water or chlorine tablets we paid the price with frequent diarrhea.

As I finished filling the canteens and started back for the house, I saw four G.I.s digging a hole next to the dead Kraut.

"We figured that since we're going to be here for a couple of days we'd bury him," one said.

New replacements, I thought to myself.

Inside the house no one had heard anything more about staying. Ayers, Marty and the others were sprawled around on the floor resting.

Still restless, I went back outside. The dead Kraut was gone and one of the G.I.s had found two pieces of wood and was trying to fit them together to make a cross. He bound the wood with a strap and stuck the fragile cross into the ground. The Krauts's I.D. card had been slipped under the strap and was fluttering in the wind.

When everyone had gone I walked over and looked at the name. It was meaningless to me, and yet, as I felt the breeze on my face I thought that a human being lay burried there who had stood on the same spot and felt the same wind just a few hours before. I wondered if he had a family, perhaps a wife and children praying for his safety. Maybe there were anxious parents, such as my own, waiting for some news. And what news would they receive? Missing in action? Would anyone ever know what happened to this man?

"Hey," Ayers called to me. "The rumor was wrong as usual. Get your stuff together. We're moving out."

As I walked along behind Ayers, I looked back at that cross which had already slipped to form an X. I was sure that the I.D. card would soon blow away in the wind.

Wine and party every night
Kill the past and still the fright
Days are destruction
Death and killing no one wants
The memory haunts
Tormenting dreams
Are endless.

"Hey Ron, more vermouth? You're going to sleep!"

The sound of Ayer's voice snaps me back to the present. He is filling my glass again, and Clemens is still talking.

"Jock here was wounded by machine gun fire in Libya," he explains.

"Yes," Jock nods. "You know that old Jerry trick. When it's night they fire the machine guns all the time. You see the tracers going out like fire balls. They aim the gun with the tracers high, but they fire another gun without tracers low. You see the tracers and think you can crawl up under them. You don't realize that other gun is firing too. That's what happened to me. They got me with the other gun."

"And when you're wounded," Clemens continues, "they send you to a hospital in Egypt. Now, if you're badly wounded your army will send you back to the states, but with us they send us to Egypt. They say things are in short supply at home and Egypt is just as good. Can you imagine? Egypt as good as Blighty?"

I sip on the vermouth and my thoughts wander back to my own hospital experience. That was when I really got to know Denny. There couldn't be a better platoon sergeant.

My skin was aflame and my eyes felt like glowing embers, I was burning up. It was a hot summer day, but we were not in the sun. Our slit trenches were scattered through an orchard of ancient olive trees that spread their massive branches overhead like a shield.

"I feel like I've had too much red wine," I said to Ayers.

"Where've you been hiding it? I haven't seen wine for days."

"I haven't had too much—I haven't had any. I just feel like I've had too much. It's like a hangover. I think I have a fever."

Ayers put his hand on my forehead, "You're sizzling man. I could heat my rations on your head. You better go to the aid station and get checked."

When Marty told me the aid station was back in the town of Palaya, I decided I didn't want to go. Seeing the cluster of buildings so far to the rear discouraged me. How could I make it over a couple of hills when I could hardly lift my feet? My head felt light and my shoulders ached.

"You'd better go before you get any sicker," Marty insisted. "Some guys have been getting malaria."

I knew he was right and the fear of malaria sent a shiver down my spine. Yet, my body was pleading to be let alone. I just wanted to stretch out on the ground.

With a sudden serge of determination I forced myself to rise and start the journey that led across the mountain ridges. My eyes were focused on a gap in the distant wall that was the gate to the town.

"Stay off the skyline," Marty yelled after me. "The Krauts can see you if you go up there."

That was bad news. It meant I couldn't follow the road. Reversing direction I stumbled down the slope of the hill until I found a trail. It was a rocky path that led me all around the hills, but never closer to Palaya. Finally I found myself below some bluffs with the town, tauntingly secure, far above me.

"To hell with it! I'll take my chances," I mumbled to myself

Walking along the dirt road was easier and Palaya began to grow larger. When I was half way to the town I heard someone yell my name and a helmet emerged from among the branches and shrubs beside the road. The face was radiant with a large smile and just to look at it made me feel better.

It was Andrews, an old buddy from the states. I hadn't seen him since our outfit was broken up and we were sent out as replacements.

Andrews was full of news about our buddies from our old division. Many of them were close by in A and B companies. Clancy and Pace were both in B company, but Clancy had been sent to the hospital with shell shock.

After a brief rent I plodded on toward Palaya, still worrying about being on the skyline, but without the strength to go any faster. When I entered the gate a large white banner with a red cross guided me to the aid station.

Inside, the room was large and austere. The only furniture was a small wooden table and two chairs. A medic was sitting at the table writing, and he hardly looked up when he asked me why I was there.

As I started to explain, he nodded and told me to sit down. Before I could say more than a few words he stuck a thermometer in my mouth and went on writing.

Suddenly I felt weak. With sweat breaking out all over my brow it took all my will power to remain sitting in the chair. My throat went dry, my breath was short and my sagging back was begging for a place to lie down. While I fought to remain conscious the medic went on writing forever.

At last he looked up and calmly pulled the thermometer out to check it. His expression indicated nothing, but he told me to go into the next room and lie down on a pad on the floor.

The room was windowless, cool and dark. Gratefully I sank to the floor. I fell into a fitful sleep, frequently awakening wanting water. Once a vague figure brought me a drink. Like a winged phantom my mind sped from one place to another, remembering past illnesses and seeing strange faces in the dark. At one time I awoke confused and looked around at the unfamiliar room. It must have been a storehouse for a church because there were gilt religious figures stacked in the corner. How long the night seemed! How I longed for the morning!

A shadowy figure appeared in the bright light of the doorway. It was calling my name, telling me to go into the other room.

When I staggered out into the blinding brightness all I could see was Sergeant Denny's red hair.

"I came to see how you're doing," he said.

The medic silenced me by pushing the thermometer into my mouth again. He then asked me when I had come to the aid station.

Seeing that a new medic was on duty, I pulled out the thermometer and told him I had come in the previous afternoon.

"That's not right," Denny said. "You just left the company a couple of hours ago."

"This aid station wasn't even here yesterday," the medic agreed.

I couldn't believe what I was hearing. Remembering the long night and the hours of thirst, the fitful sleep and dreams, and the longing for the morning to come, I could only shake my head.

"Your mind is playing tricks on you," the medic said.

He checked the thermometer again and then told me to go back into the other room and lie down, which I did gladly. Closing my eyes once more, I could hear Denny and the medic talking quietly.

It was early evening when the medic called me out again and told me to notify my company that I was going to the hospital.

"Can I use the phone?" I asked.

"We have no field phones to the company areas," he said.

In a confused state I wandered out and headed for the company. Nothing looked familiar and I walked among the hills for over an hour. I developed a nagging fear that I might step on a mine on the unfamiliar trail. I grew alarmed when some barefoot Italians fled past me in fright. When I saw a group of dirty, tired looking G.I.s in the distance, I felt sure I was lost.

Every way I turned seemed to be the wrong way, until suddenly I was walking under huge gnarled olive trees. I had accidentally stumbled into the company area.

"What are you doing here?" Denny asked.

"I came back to tell you I'm going to the hospital," I said. "You shouldn't be walking around," he said. "I know. I've got to get back."

"Well stay off the skyline. It's especially hazardous at sunset," he reminded me.

I heard him, but I was so weak and miserable, and afraid of getting lost again, that I followed the road back to the town. "Where the hell have you been? the medic demanded angrily when he saw me. We've been looking all over for you."

"You told me to tell my company I was going to the hospital," I reminded him in a half dead voice. "It was a long ways."

"I didn't know it was so far," his voice softened. "The others have already started. The ambulance is waiting down the hill."

He tied a card to the button hole in my shirt and pointed to several bandaged men and four medics who were carrying a wounded man on a litter.

I couldn't catch up with them. I was at the end of my energy, and no matter how I tried to move faster I got farther behind. The medics reached the ambulance and loaded the wounded man, and I was still fifty yards away. They watched and waited patiently as I closed the gap. I hardly remembered the rough ride to the hospital.

"I must be dead and this is heaven," I thought. There was a cot under me instead of damp ground, a pillow under my head instead of a helmet, pajamas on my body instead of a hot wool uniform, and there was music instead of gunfire.

Suddenly I was receiving a lot of personal attention. An enlisted man is not used to such things. The nurses were cheerful and friendly and the chaplain's assistant, Corporal Afton, spent hours talking with me. Even the doctor showed a careful interest in my chart, asking questions and ordering blood tests.

The hospital ward was a large pyramidal tent. The canvas sides had been rolled up to let the summer day flow in, so we were able to look out at the fields of golden grain. In the distance a strange peak rose above the hills, standing out like a beacon. Topping the peak were walls and buildings with the appearance of a fairy castle.

The test for malaria came out negative, and since my temperature was coming down no one worried about the cause of my illness.

A nurse told us that there had been some members of the Japanese-American battalion in the hospital and it had been hard to keep them there. They were eager to get back into action.

The men on either side of me didn't feel that way and neither did I. We had found a piece of America in an alien land where we could relax and listen to our favorite music broadcast by Fifth Army in the Field. As a voice crooned "I'll get by" I could close my eyes without fear and let my mind drift home. The music was soothing and healing. I was dancing again at the Hollywood Palladium or lying on the sand at Hermosa Beach. The war was a bad dream and I was finally waking up.

Each day I grew stronger and Corporal Afton continued to visit with me. His duties required him to write letters to the families of the men who were wounded, and after I had written my own letters I helped him with his tremendous job. I didn't realize he was also writing to my mother.

Being in the hospital gave us a chance to renew our contacts with family and friends by mail.

July 23, 1944

Dear Mother, Dad, Gladys,

I'm sending this by V-mail so you should get it faster. I'm terribly sorry I've been unable to write more often, but I've been in action at the front and of course there's little time. I have a touch of the flu or something—at any rate I have a temperature, so I'm resting in the hospital. I feel better now.

My mail has been mixed up but my change of address is probably responsible for that.

Everyone is watching the Russian gains eagerly, and I for one hope they get this over with soon. I've been thinking a lot about you as I lay here. It's going to be wonderful to see you all again. That's about all I look forward to.

When I get back to America I want to stay there and travel no more. Over here one learns to appreciate a fellow American. You never saw such friendliness as they show to each other.

Please be careful, and I'll be seeing you soon.

Love to you all,
Ron

FIVE

We all looked fresh and sharp in our clean uniforms with neatly creased pants. When we had arrived at the hospital our clothing was the color of the fine dust that covered the roads and trails, and our faces were streaked with dirt and salty perspiration that had accumulated during many hot days in the field. Now we were being discharged and told that it was each man's personal responsibility to find his way back to his own company.

No one knew exactly how to do this. The line companies were always moving and not even the clerks in the hospital knew their locations. I stood in front of the hospital with the other discharged patients doing what the army had taught us to do best, waiting patiently.

Using the shade of the large, green pyramidal tent to shield me from the sun, I watched the ambulances and trucks that were coming and going, hoping to see a vehicle from my division. I was not anxious or in a hurry, for I assumed my company was still at the front.

It seemed a haphazard way of returning a man from the hospital, but as sometimes happens in the army, things worked out amazingly well. I caught a ride on a medical truck that took me to my division headquarters.

There I waited at the motor pool scanning the bumpers of the vehicles. When I saw a communication jeep from my regiment the driver was glad to give me a ride.

He desperately needed someone to talk to, and after he told me that my whole division was off the front and in a rear area I was content to silently listen to his monologue. He was telling me all about his home and his girl while the wheels of the jeep spun dust into the thirsty fields and orchards.

We rode in the shade of the tall trees that lined the dirt road. The branches mingled overhead so we seemed to be traveling through a tunnel.

The ride ended dramatically when the driver wheeled off the road and started overland through some orchards.

"The companies in your battalion are scattered around here," he said.

A spot of red caught my eye, the short red hair of a man without a helmet.

"This is it!" I told him. "Those men are in my platoon."

The brakes of the jeep sent a cloud of dust through the area, but no one seemed to mind.

"Welcome back," Denny grinned.

Smiling faces crowded around me. They were like Robin's men in Sherwood forest. It was time for chow, so Marty got me a mess kit. Ayers invited me to share his pup tent and Wallace brought me a mug of coffee.

How different things were from what I had imagined. We sat around on the ground talking and laughing as we waited for the metal coffee cups to cool so we wouldn't burn our lips. There was a circle of radiant faces with smiling eyes. These were not the same faces I had known at the front a short time before when these same men were silent machines going methodically about their duties, cunning animals with every instinct alert for survival.

I had dreaded returning to the company, unaware of the common bonds that had been established and how quickly I had been accepted. Also, as my buddies had apparently learned to do, I was accepting the present and tuning out the future and the past. There was hot food, a place to sleep and we were off the front.

"We'll be out of action for an indefinite time," Marty said.

"That's the good news, but now hear the bad," Ayers said. "We're here for training. We're going to attack across the Arno river. The Krauts are dug in on the North bank and the only way across is to make an amphibious assault."

"Lucky us," Wallace added.

This was not a rumor. The training was serious. During the daytime we followed the same old routine of exercise and practicing mock attacks, but at night we worked on the planned attack across the Arno river.

Each morning started out with a hike as a different officer led the entire battalion through the local countryside. Morale was high since there was no fear of enemy snipers, but we hated it when the long legged lieutenant from A company led the way. Our company was then at the end of the line and for some strange reason we were all running to keep up.

When we returned to our base we broke up into platoons and played capture the hill. Denny would walk ahead giving hand signals and the three squads responded and advanced to the top. On different days we attacked the hill from a variety of places.

When Sarvo, the platoon guide, went with our squad we could feel the tension between him and Marty.

"They've been rivals all through training," Martin explained to us. "Both were always bucking for rank, each trying to be top dog."

"It's a good thing they're both staffs," Ayers said. "I don't think they could be in the same platoon if one was higher than the other."

The good times were the afternoons when we were free to do as we liked. We could sleep, write letters, or wander through the nearby village of Villa Magna. We had also learned to appreciate the simple pleasures of washing and shaving with hot water, and we even cut each others hair.

The style was short all over. It wasn't the handsome style of the German soldiers with their long wavy hair, but it was pactical since we wore helmets most of the time and had little chance to wash our heads at the front.

The one thing we did not get enough of was sleep. We were not back from the front for a rest, and night after night, as soon as it was dark we would walk silently down to a small stream about a mile from the camp. Row boats were hidden among the shrubs along the water's edge.

Denny and Marty were whispering for us to be quiet, but it wasn't quiet. When we pulled the boats from their hiding places the branches cracked and snapped as they brushed against the sides of the boats. There were always splashing sounds as we waded into the water.

Ayers was on one side of the boat and I was on the other. We slowly pushed the boat into the cool water until we were waist deep. Then, joined by four others, we rolled over the sides of the boat, picked up the paddles and worked our way slowly to the opposite bank. When we neared the other bank we again entered the water and waded ashore.

Night after night we practiced this simple operation, and every time my apprehension grew. Every splash of the water seemed deafening. It didn't seem possible to pull this off without being detected. At the slightest sound in the night the Krauts would shoot up a flare, and as these hung in the sky they lit up the landscape like daylight.

Occasionally we were given a night off from the tense repetition. Then we all sat on the slope of a hill and watched a movie projected against the white wall of the house at battalion headquarters. For a few hours we were back in America caught up in different lives.

One night the show was interrupted by the familiar drone of a German plane. The projector was shut off and we sat listening in the dark. No bombs were dropped and the noise gradually faded away. The war had come back.

A traveling U.S.O. show arrived one afternoon complete with American girls in flashy costumes. They sang, told jokes and danced while we crowded together on the hillside like kids at our first circus.

When one of the girls was going through her dance routine a column of tanks rumbled down the road behind her. Whirling, she kicked high over her head toward the men in the tanks, and with a loud "clunk" one of the tanks broke down. This brought clapping, whistles and cheers.

"Send her to the front to kick at the Jerry tanks !"

Marty had been called to a morning meeting and in the afternoon he led the squad out on a hillside to a spot in the shade of a giant tree.

"Sit down," he said. "The officers think we should have a discussion.

"It seems that morale in Italy is pretty low. A lot of the men feel that the fighting here is not important. All the publicity now is about the fighting in France, and Italy has become a forgotten front.

"Captain Mathews thinks we should have a talk to remind us why we are fighting and what's important. Would someone like to start the discussion?"

There were no volunteers. Everyone sat silently. After about a minute Marty thought he should say something himself.

"Well, the way I look at it is.......the U.S. didn't ask for this war, and now that we have it someone has to fight. I feel that it's as much my duty as anyone else's."

No one else spoke. Most of the men nodded and that ended the discussion.

The rumor was going around that when there was no moon we would move up to cross the river. After that, as we paddled across the water we looked at the moon, noting the phases. Like condemned men we watched the shrinking moon and feared the approaching inevitable assault.

The morning sun usually drove the fears from our minds and during our free time we again accepted the joys of the present. We wandered through the village and around the countryside, making friends with some of the Italian civilians.

How strange it seemed to see civilian families living in houses, working and playing together as we had once done. It seemed out of script and not possible in this alien land of war and devastation.

Women from the village carried large baskets of clothes on their heads as they passed us on their way to the stream to do their laundry. Their laughter and chatter drifted up to us as we watched them rubbing the clothes in the water and spreading them out on the rocks.

The farmers working in the fields waved to us, and one man invited Pollack and me into his house for a glass of wine.

Pollack was a good friend and buddy who had been in my communications section in the states. He was lucky enough to be assigned as a radio man at our battalion headquarters. When I returned from the hospital I discovered we were in the same area. After that we spent hours together exploring the countryside.

The man who invited us in was a friendly host, but one who knew no English. However, my school Latin was adequate for communication. The woman explained that they didn't speak Italian, they spoke Tuscana and it was closer to the original Latin.

There were two children in the family, a girl eight and a boy ten. The boy was an altar boy at the church. This interested Pollack, and since he was Catholic he wanted to visit the church.

This pleased our host and he invited us both to go with them on Sunday. He told us he was a church official of some kind and the house they lived in belonged to the church. He also took us over to see another house, one that he owned and rented out.

Sunday was a beautiful summer day and Pollack and I had one of the most peaceful days we could remember. The church was a small building over five hundred years old with thick adobe walls that had been covered with white plaster and capped with a red tile roof. Inside there were rows of wooden benches and a beautiful gilded altar with many candles.

I did not know the procedures and did not kneel when the parishioners did, but everyone was friendly and seemed pleased that Pollack and I had attended their services.

As we walked slowly back to the village with our Italian host he pointed out the damage caused by the war. A German half-track, wrecked and burned black, rested near the church. The mausoleum at the cemetary had been hit by artillery fire. The walls were blown apart and the skeletons were hanging out in grotesque positions. That mausoleum held the remains of Italian soldiers killed in the first world war, the war to end wars.

During the recent fighting a group of tiger tanks had used the church as a shield and shelled the village from the churchyard.

When our hosts invited us into their house again and gave us fruit and wine, I felt we should give them something in return, but Pollack and I were both empty handed. Reaching into my pocket I felt the small change I had brought with me from the states.

I had two silver dimes, and when I offered them to the boy and the girl their faces beamed with joy. The father admired the winged mercury head on the coins and said he would have them made into jewelry. They had no silver, for Mussolini had asked them to turn in all their gold and silver jewelry to pay for the electrical system.

As we walked back through the village, Pollack and I stopped to buy some pears from an old woman who had set up a stand. We sat on a wall and looked out at the green hills covered with fig and olive trees. It was so peaceful that I wanted time to stand still. I couldn't think of the future.

>And through them we see our past
>In a world that didn't last
>When we felt love
>And knew what it was to touch
>We miss it much
>Caught in a total war
>That's endless.

Back at camp Ayers invited me to a chicken dinner. Wallace had found a chicken running around and had cooked it. One chicken for the whole squad wasn't much, but we all had a taste.

At first I thought it was the goose that Truett and Scotty had caught the week before. Scotty had tied a rope around its leg and tied it to a tree. The idea was to fatten it up for a future feast. We had all been feeding it scraps of food.

Whenever anyone asked if the goose was fat enough yet, the consensus was that we should wait awhile longer. We would have it on a special occasion.

The best part of being off the front was mail call. Our letters were catching up with us, and we also had time to answer them. I received letters from my family and high school friends. Four girls wrote to me when I first went into the service. By the time I finished my training and had a furlough home one of them was married and the one I had dated last had a steady boy friend. Another was a good friend's sister and wrote to me as a family friend. The fourth one, Lisa, continued to write to me regularly telling me of her college classes and social activities.

Very few of the men in our squad received letters from girl friends. One by one they received "Dear John" letters from their girls. The war put pressure on the girls tool

No one in the squad was married—we were all quite young.

When writing we used V-mail forms that could be sent on microfilm. These reached home faster. There was so little we could write because our company officers read, signed and censored everything. We had trouble filling up the small sheet.

August 6, 1944

Dear Mother, Dad, Gladys,

Today is Sunday again so I attended the services by our chaplain. The bells of the local Catholic church rang out over the hills and the Italians were dressed up and the children scrubbed pink.

The hills are taking on a brown burned look from the summer sun, although some of the fields are still green.

We went to a show last night and saw "The Heat's On," with Mae West. Many Italians came from the village to sit on the hill and watch. There are children everywhere, and some of them are cute. A little girl was standing in the street crying so one of the fellows stopped and gave her a life-saver. We left her blinking and eating it.

Well, be careful and write soon,

All My Love,
Ron

July 21, 1944

Dear Son,

I didn't get to write yesterday because Dad had the day off. He hasn't had a day off for some time and has been working overtime every day. I suggested we go somewhere to have a good time, so we went to Hollywood to dinner and a show. We saw Deanna Durbin in "His Butler's Sister." The Pantages is a beautiful theater. We window shopped for a while.

It was a good thing we went out because they told Dad they had called him seventeen times trying to get him to work.

While we were out there I bought the record "Cherry." Betty wanted us to get it. It is by Harry James and is very pretty. Have you heard it?

Glady's sailor friend was over last night again. His ship hasn't left yet. He sewed a button on his coat while he was here --what a life! He has three stars on his ribbon--you know what that means.

I haven't had any horse meat for four days and Kitty won't eat anything else. Dad is going to get a pound of butter today. You know one pound is sixteen points.

Well, this is all I can think of this time. Now take good care of yourself and don't catch any cold.

With Lots of Love,
Mother

August 13, 1944

Dear Mother, Dad, Gladys,

I'm sitting here in the shade of a fig tree by a grape arbor, but neither the figs or the grapes are ripe. The Italians use every bit of ground to grow things. There will be a corn field with fig trees and olive trees around it and grape vines under the trees. They terrace the steep hills and plant everything.

The other day Pollack and I talked to some Italians by using Latin and sign language. We were able to understand each other pretty well and they are anxious to help you learn the language.

We learned a lot about how the people live. The schools are not free and it costs a lot to send the children to school. Most of the farm land in a district is held by one man, called a padrone. All the farmers work for him in kind of a feudal system-

The farmers all have heard that American farms are mechanized and they marvel at the use of tractors and combines.

I've been reading lately and finished the book, 'High Wind" I'm now readinc one about the New England fishing grounds called "Ringed Horizon." Reading is the best way to relax here. I just wish I had more time for it. Right now I'm usually lucky just to get my correspondence caught up.

The most important thing in my life right now is the letters I get. The news is looking a little better. Maybe I'll see you all before too long.

All My Love,
Ron

July 10, 1944

Dear Ron,

Surprise--a letter! I don't know where the time goes. It seems like nothing gets done anymore. Yesterday Tommy came over—he got a pass. So I had that rare thing known as a date.

Yesterday we got off work at 4:00 to go to the Firestone Broadcast. It was pretty good—classical music sung by Richard Crooks. After that one of the girls knew of a real good place to get hot fudge Sundays so we walked from NBC up past Graumans Chinese which is about fifteen blocks—and when we got there they were out of ice cream. After recovering from a state of shock and hysterics we ordered a beat up, puny sandwich. Then I went over to Margaret's house for dinner and spent the night. She's a. kick! We talked and talked until 12:00 and I thought I was going to have to stuff a pillow down her throat so I could get some sleep. She's the best natured thing you ever saw.

Mother and I went up to Germains last week and we saw the cutest dog. He was half airdale and half cocker. He had bushy eyebrows and whiskers that stuck straight out. He looked at you out of the corner of his eye. He had such character—I wanted him so bad. It gets so lonesome around here and a dog is good company.

We got the record "Cherry" by Harry James and it sure is pretty. I just love it—in fact I think it's my favorite, but it's no good unless Harry James plays it.

Guess what I walked all over town for? Imagine, a jig-saw puzzle. Well, I figured Mother would get weary of working the same old one and I looked everywhere—and do you know, I couldn't find one. I guess they don't make them anymore.

Well, take good care of yourself and be careful. I'll write again soon.

Lots of Love,
Gladys

It was a perfect summer evening, but in the distance we saw rows of moving lights, the eyes of gray monsters coming toward us.

"They may be supply trucks," Wallace said.

"That many supply trucks? Coming here?" Martin asked. "We never needed that many supplies before."

Deep down we all knew what was happening, but no one had the courage to say it. All of our wishful thinking was shattered when the order came to strike tents and prepare to move.

"Do you think we're going to the Arno?" Malik asked.

"Where else?" Marty answered.

"There goes our goose dinner," Scotty said. "I might as well turn the bird loose."

"We'd never have eaten him anyhow," Ayers said.

I knew he was right. The goose had become a pet, and we all knew it wanted to live as much as we did.

As we boarded the trucks I had visions of wading into cold, black water while mortar shells exploded around us and machine guns sprayed firey tracers from the north bank of the Arno river.

SIX

We were huddled together resting on each other with our army blankets draped over us, for we were conditioned to sleep anywhere, even on the jarring, swaying wooden benches in the back of the truck. We had learned not to anticipate anything and had trained our minds not to think. We let the humming motor tranquilize us, but when it stopped we were instantly awake.

"O.K.," a voice called out of the night, "everybody out of the trucks."

The long ride was over, but where were we? It was so dark that I couldn't see the ground as I followed my buddies and jumped from the truck.

"It looks like we'll be walking the rest of the way," Ayers said.

"How far is the line?" I asked aloud, not expecting an answer.

"Bring your shelter halves with you," the voice in the night ordered. "We'll be making camp here."

So, it was not the front! You didn't pitch tents at the front. Yet, I could hear Kraut machine guns firing in the distance.

"Where the hell are we?" Ayers yelled. "And where's the damned river?"

"Near Florence," an answer came back. "You'll see the Arno in the morning."

Relieved that we were not going into action at once, we stumbled around in the dark trying to get our pup tents set up before something happened to change the orders. Spreading a blanket on the ground,

Ayers and I crawled under the canvas and stretched out. Accepting gratefully the hand fate had delt us we were instantly asleep.

"Hey, look at this bitchin sight!" Ayers called out.

Looking out I was stunned by the panorama of roofs, domes and spires that lay below us. Where there had been only darkness, the morning light revealed a picture from the renaissance. Buildings stretched for miles on each side of the river. However, it was easy to see that Florence was a divided city. Her many bridges were dead animals with broken backs, their spans sunk into the deep water of the river. They were a reminder to us of our reason for being there.

Our camp was beginning to look like the one we had just left at Villa Magna. The cooks set up a kitchen and pup tents were scattered all over the hillside. Once again we were in an ancient olive orchard.

The nearby farmhouse had the appearance of a wealthy estate. The white two story building with its bright, red tile roof sat on top of the hill surrounded by shrubbery and tall cypress trees. Its windows, like arrogant eyes, looked down on the city below.

Without warning a savage blast shocked us from our tranquility! Dust and flying debris were hurled out from the center of the company area. The kitchen was shattered. The Kraut artillery had sent us a rude calling card to arouse us from our lethargy.

"To the other side of the hill!" Captain Mathews called out. "Move everything to the other side."

"There goes our view," Martin said.

"We have a view, they have a view," Denny added.

"It's not quite like Villa Magna," I commented.

"Florence is an open city," Denny explained to us. "Both sides have agreed there will be no fighting there in order to preserve the art treasures."

So there were still some civilized people left in the world! It seemed out of character in modern Europe.

"If there's no fighting, where in the hell is the artillery that just fired on us?" Wallace asked.

With our camp moved to the other side of the hill we felt secure from the enemy artillery, but we didn't know what else to expect.

There was a constant flow of rumors about crossing the Arno, yet day after day we just sat and waited.

Our only daytime duty was to take turns standing guard, for many guards were posted around our camp and we were not allowed outside the area. To our surprise, our officers were beginning to act like we were in garrison, expecting us to look like state side soldiers. We were ordered to be clean shaven and neat, and although the weather was hot we were not allowed to carry canteens with us on our guard duty.

"I haven't been without a canteen since I've been over here," Ayers complained. "It's a hell of a thing! Now that we're back where there's plenty of water we have to stand out there for hours without a drink."

When it was my turn for guard duty I was lucky. Denny made me a corporal of the guard and it was my duty to march the men to their posts and bring those relieved back. Also, I was to check the posts every hour. Remembering Ayer's complaint, I carried a canteen with me and gave every man a drink.

With lots of free time we were able to write many letters. This meant we would be getting answers in the future. It was like building a bank account. Letters were our contact with the world and our life blood.

We also had time to read. Our PX ration came in giving us candy, beer and paper back books.

There was one book all the men in our squad carried, a copy of the New Testament or the Catholic prayer book. I carried my New Testament in my shirt pocket. It was given to me at a U.S.O. club and had a card in the front of it that read, "This book is a gift to you from S.S. Class #19, St. Luke's E.&R. Church, Lock Haven, Penn."

I also carried a copy of the Pocket Book of Verse.

To pass the time I sketched pictures of the surrounding scenery. I sent a drawing of the stately farmhouse with its Cypress tree sentries home on a V-mail, but I didn't know if it would pass the censors.

Although Florence was an open city to be spared by both sides, we weren't sure what this meant. During the daytime everything was quiet and the citizens seemed to be going peace-fully about their business, but at night we could hear machine gun and rifle fire from all over the city. According to our patrols the streets were a black jungle in a lightless city.

We were on the southern edge, in the hills, looking down on the entire city, and the Germans were in the northern suburbs. The city between the opposing armies was a no man's land. At night patrols from both sides entered the city and all night the streets were ravaged by firing from rifles, machine guns and mortars. Every intersection was a potential booby trap.

One reason for sending out patrols was to capture enemy soldiers for questioning. No one knew what to expect and each side was probing the strengths of the other. We soon learned to dread the coming of night.

"Patrol tonight! Patrol tonight! Patrol tonight!" The dreaded words passed from mouth to mouth. A patrol was sent out from our company every night, twelve men with automatic weapons. There were no volunteers so the men were chosen from a different platoon each time by rotation.

The missions and objectives changed each night, and each day we listened to the tales of terrifying experiences told by the returning men. We listened with fascination and dread as they told of fire fights in dark alleys and of searching through musty wine cellars in the blackness of night. Booby traps, foot mines, and ambushes could await anywhere in the lightless buildings.

"We were in this warehouse among all these crates," Scotty said, "and we could hear people moving around bumping into things. There could be Jerries all around us. It was blacker than hell in there."

"They're nothing but suicide squads," Ayers said. And who could disagree with him.

It was the first platoon's turn for patrol and it would be a tough one. G-2 wanted more information, so the objective of the patrol was to capture some Krauts alive and bring them back for questioning.

All afternoon the men prepared, putting netting over their helmets to hide any reflections, cleaning their weapons and checking out grenades.

At dusk, after the evening meal, a small six wheeled truck crept into the area and the twelve men climbed aboard. The sergeant in charge made a last minute inspection of each man, checking to be sure that each had two bandoliers of ammo and two hand grenades. Everyone carried an automatic weapon. Lieutenant James gave the final inspection.

"Your patrol will last all night," he told them. "You're going out to pick up some Krauts, but remember the Krauts will be out doing the same. They'll be after you. We know they've been coming across the Arno, and there's only one place they can cross easily. You'll set up an ambush, but if they get across first, you know what that means. Good Luck!"

We all remembered that a patrol was sent to the same area the previous night. The mission was to search the buildings along the river. All hell broke loose with mortars firing from empty buildings and machine guns firing down the streets. There were Kraut road blocks at key intersections. That's the way it was at night.

No one ever saw the Krauts crossing the river and we suspected they hid their weapons and stayed in the area disguised as Italians.

As the truck began to move forward we all called out to the men, "Good luck! Stay alert!"

They waved and nodded, but their faces were serious.

When the truck had taken the men as far as it dared, the patrol continued on foot. No words were spoken, for absolute silence was imperative as they moved into the city, but it was also necessary that they not lose contact with each other in the dark. That would be a disaster and could erupt into a fire fight among themselves.

On the cobblestone streets their shoes made no noise, an advantage over the German hob nailed boots. In the distance the sounds of war were already echoing through the city, the speedy fire of the German machine pistols answered by the chug chug of the American B.A.R.s. Occasionally lines of tracers, like speeding fireflies, leaped out from the far bank of the river. Some trigger happy Jerry!

As the patrol neared the selected spot near the river, the men's nerves grew taut. They would soon know if they had arrived before the Krauts. The staff sergeant in charge slowed the pace and moved cautiously forward.

Without warning the rattle of a machine pistol exploded the silence and fiery tracers danced all around. Instinctively, and simultaneously, all the men dropped to the ground, but the sergeant doubled up and rolled over.

Seeing their leader hit, the next two men reached out an grabbed his legs, pulling him back behind a low wall. The Krauts were closing in, firing from two sides. The American patrol was badly outnumbered.

The Krauts were hurling their potato masher grenades and calling out in English for the Americans to surrender. The voices were coming from all directions and getting closer.

The wounded sergeant was shot in both legs and couldn't get up. Breaking his silence he ordered his men to pull back and get out of there.

"Not without you," they told him.

The Krauts were on three sides and closing in.

"You can't make it with me," the sergeant told the men.

"Yes, we can. We'll carry you."

"No! No! Go on!"

Looking at the determined faces next to him, the sergeant turned his head away. Without warning he placed the gun to his head and pulled the trigger.

The stunned men, with Kraut bullets flying all around them, crawled backward firing their automatic weapons at the pursuing Germans. Leaping and racing to the rear they were soon swallowed up by the black maze around them. They escaped the trap with only one casualty.

It was the following day when a German party, under a flag of truce, returned the sergeant's body. They had seen and understood what happened.

"We want to return the body of a brave man."

For three weeks we continued the nightly patrols. All along the front the intelligence sections were gathering information. A plan would be formulated and we would have to make the dreaded assault across the river.

The days were quiet and the weather remained pleasant. We stayed inside our posted area and continued to read and play cards. We had been in one place long enough to start receiving some mail.

August 2, 1944

Dear Son,

The weather has been warm so we worked in the victory garden yesterday. Gladys planted the rows of vegetables and they all came up crooked. It looks awful but I guess it won't affect the growing.

Dad is working overtime tonight so he won't be home for dinner. I am going to town to meet Gladys after work and we are going to dinner and to a show. Wish you were here to go with us.

Haven't much news—everything is about the same only everything seems to be getting scarcer all the time. I have every-thing accumulated to make you some cookies now. I am going to make them tomorrow. I've been looking for some good apples and oranges too. I don't know where everything is going.

Gladys sent packages to two boys in the Pacific. She saw their names in the paper. They had a list of service men who had relatives to write to them.

She had a date with a sailor last night and when he brought her home she gave him Dad's beer. When Dad got up he had a fit --but you know Gladys.

Kitty just got up and walked across my letter so if there are cat hairs on it it's his fault. He's sitting looking at me. He probably wants his horse meat.

Dad and I went to the Legion meeting Tuesday night and the president wasn't there. Do you know they made me be president for that night. They just handed me a book and told me to read out of it how to lead. Was I glad when the meeting was over.

I am putting your letters away and will keep them for you.

Well, this is about everything I can think of this time. Everything is as dead as ever. If you want anything just tell me. Take care of yourself,

With Lots of Love,
Mother

P.S. Betty is moving back home since they are sending Charles over seas. The army eliminated A.S.T.P. and he was transferred to the infantry.

We had a special luxury, the company radio. We could listen to the news from the B.B.C. and music from Fifth Army in the Field. Sometimes we even tuned in to Axis Sally. We knew her German version of the news was propaganda, but we enjoyed the music. In the past she had been useful when she read out the names of captured Americans. When she announced the sinking of an American ship in the Pacific she claimed it went down with all hands lost. Such an announcement was followed by the playing of "How Deep is the Ocean."

There was no repeat of the shelling by the Kraut artillery, but the cooks created some explosions of their own. Whenever they needed a new hole for dumping garbage, instead of digging one they put a charge in the ground and blew a crater.

"Fire in the hole," one of them would cry.

This was followed by a blast that showered the camp with dirt and rock. It fell all over like rain.

Of course we spent part of our free time cleaning, oiling and caring for our weapons, for we knew we could be called upon at any time to use them and a jammed weapon could cost a man his life. However, cleaning a weapon could be dangerous too.

A shot rang out! A bullet hit the man beside me in the chest, but ricocheted off and burried itself in the ground.

A private from the second platoon rushed over to the man who was hit.

"I was cleaning my tommy gun," he stammered. His eyes were scared, his face ashen. "I didn't think it was loaded."

The man who was hit reached into his shirt pocket and pulled out his copy of the New Testament. The book had a metal cover, and there was a dent in the center.

The order came! We must be ready to move in an hour! We were puzzled because it was morning and the sun was high in the sky.

"I know we're not crossing the Arno by daylight," Marty said.

"We're leaving by truck," Denny said. "They may be hauling us to a different sector."

"And then we'll wait until it's dark," Ayers added.

No one really knew what was happening, but we climbed aboard the trucks expecting anything.

We weren't kept guessing for long. Lieutenant James gave us the latest word. The British had thrown a baily bridge across the river and we were going to rush as much across it as we could. It was our job to provide infantry protection on the other side of the Arno.

The trucks roared down the hill and rushed across the narrow bridge that floated on pontoons. We were right in the middle of Florence, and once across the river we left the trucks and started out, single file, walking north.

Suddenly we were among the ancient buildings we had been watching from the hills. On we walked, block after block, past the ancient cathedral and museums and past the red light district.

The prostitutes yelled and waved from the windows and the G.I.s cheered and waved back. I wondered how recently the Krauts had been there. Had the girls just waved goodby to Kraut lovers?

Where were the Germans? We continued without stopping hour after hour, through the city streets and into the suburbs. There was not one Kraut to be seen.

In the afternoon the sun was warm and our morale was rising. It was as if a weight had been lifted from our heads. We were at last across the Arno, and with no casualties.

The more we realized how lucky we were the happier we became. We were all smiling and joking. Scotty, Malik, Ayers Rule, Truett, Marty and everyone else was talking. It was infectious!

"We trained for weeks to cross the Arno, and then we rode across on trucks!" Wallace shouted.

"Yea, for the British!"

"This is one hell of a place for a party," Martin says, as he plops down beside Ayers. "You British know how to live. You're lucky to be staying here instead of out in a pup tent."

"Well, why not?" Everet replies. "You Yanks treat these Italians too well. Remember, they declared war on us. I don't see why you're living out in the field when there are all these buildings around."

"It's army policy not to disturb the local population," I explain. "Although at the front we often occupy buildings, but usually the people have fled."

"Before we came here we spent a week in a farm house," Martin adds. "It was just beyond Florence. The family stayed with their farm so we all shared the house."

"That must have been cozy," Everet smiles. "We got to know the people," I continue. "Nice family." My thoughts returned to those recent experiences and the strange phase of the war after the fall of Florence.

Families trying to survive
Happy just to be alive
Watching savage
War destroying farm and field
There is no shield
They face the fight
That's endless.

SEVEN

"Who gets the bed?" That was the question we all asked.

Not only did our squad have a modern town house to itself, but there was a large upstairs bedroom with a double bed. The box springs and matress looked new.

We walked eleven kilometers north of Florence and entered the town of Campi in full battle formation expecting to drive the Germans out, but we were greeted only by silence.

It was eerie and unreal, for in the entire town there was no sign of a human being. Like some ancient archaeological site, the modern town stood silent and deserted. We tried to imagine what people recently left there. The stores, houses and new cinema building were ghostly relics. There were shoes and clothing in the windows of the modern stores, but no footsteps or voices echoed in the downtown streets.

In the houses there was evidence everywhere of many hasty departures. Clothing was scattered about in the bedrooms and toilet articles were still in the modern bathrooms. The citizens had fled this affluent town more rapidly than the ancient inhabitants of Pompeii rushed to escape the lava from Vesuvius.

It was an uneventful hike from Florence. We walked along the highway single file with our rifles at sling arms. The weather was sunny and warm. We saw very few people, but when some girls rode by on bicycles we waved and shouted greetings to them. A few voices called out to them as if they were prostitutes, "Quanta costa?"

After searching through the town we received an order to bed down for the night, but there was still one bothersome question. Where were the Germans?

Marty was standing looking at the bed. None of us had slept in a bed for months and we all knew how luxurious it would feel to sink into those soft springs. Should we draw straws, or would Marty pull rank on us?

The house had been stripped of most of its posessions and the large mirror on the stairway was broken. This puzzled me, for many of the glass storefronts were also smashed. How did all this happen when there had been no fighting here? Did the Krauts vandelize the town as they pulled out?

On the stairway, by the broken mirror, there was a small rosary with blue beads. I was holding it in my hand studying it when Denny stuck his head in the door.

"Don't get comfortable. We're moving out." "I knew it!" Ayers said. "Somebody knew we had a bed." "They got a bunch of tanks across the river and they want infantry to protect them," Denny explained. "We'll be setting up advanced outposts."

It was twilight already, and once more we were walking north. We followed a dirt road for several miles and were once more in the country. Since it was getting dark, the captain ordered us to stop and dig slit trenches in a field. Before I could begin, Lieutenant Lyons came over and asked me to take three men and locate the other companies in our battalion that were somewhere to the east of us.

"We'll have to know everyone's position for the night."

With the new order I saw any chance of getting some sleep slip away, and the thought of going into the unknown drove all other thoughts from my mind. A patrol trying to make contact with other units along the fluid front ran many risks. Not only was there the danger of running into the enemy, but in the dim twilight other Americans could mistake us for Krauts. There was also an excellent chance we could get lost in the unfamiliar terrain, especially if we were out a long time and ended up stumbling around in the dark.

The four of us held a council and decided the most dangerous route would be by the road. Where the vanished Krauts had gone was still a mystery, but they were likely to be watching the roads. Cutting across the fields was also dangerous since we ran the risk of hitting a mine field or encountering an unseen obstacle, or even entrenched Krauts. We finally decided to follow the dusty ruts of a wagon trail that led to the east.

This rough trail took us toward a cluster of buildings where we saw some men walking around. Dropping to the ground we studied these soldiers' helmets until we were sure they were G.I.s. We continued on, trying to approach the buildings by walking normally. We didn't want to alarm anyone!

It was a piece of luck, for the men were from B Company. They directed us down the road to where their company was digging in for the night. Right along side of them A Company had set up a position, so our mission was quickly completed. However, as we had feared it was already dark.

We didn't want to return by the way we had come. It was always wise to vary your route in case you had been observed. A sniper could be waiting.

A path that led west from the A Company area seemed the best choice. Running along in the moonlight we were able to follow the path, but it was too dark to see any familiar landmarks in the distance. Soon we began to worry that we had gone too far and the moon indicated we were angling toward the north.

We could see a row of trees to our left that marked the road, and we felt certain it led back to our company area. In desperation we left the path and cut across the field to the trees.

We all agreed we were north of the company in Kraut territory. We had to follow the road going south. Running along in the dust I was once more a fearful animal with all my senses keenly alert. Every tree or shrub could conceal an enemy soldier.

Beside the road there was a house. It was dark and looked' deserted, but was in a threatening position right next to the road. The Krauts liked to hide in buildings and we knew this one had not been checked.

Jogging along, we stayed across the road from the house, but just as we were opposite it the silence was shattered. Something fell to the floor inside the building. At top speed we sprinted on down the road.

When we reached our company area again, I found Ayers had not started the slit trench. He had been sent to the rear to pick up some rations and had just returned himself.

I picked up the shovel, but it seemed useless. Clouds had covered the moon and it was starting to rain. In the distance the lightning flashed as the fast moving storm raced toward us.

Wallace and Malik had crawled under the low branches of a large bush and they called for us to join them. It was dryer, and huddled together it was warmer, but I was still shivering in my wet clothes and slept very little.

Just before sunrise, with the moon still in the sky, we started moving again. The air was refreshing after the rain and as we walked along the road the early rays of the sun began touching the top leaves of the trees that lined our way.

We saw the farmhouse by the road that had looked so sinister the night before, and we realized how lucky we had been when the door flew open and five gray clad Jerries raced out and around the house.

When we reached the building it was deserted and all signs of the Krauts had vanished.

Continuing down the road several kilometers, we came to another farm. There the company was divided.

"We're going to scatter through the area and set up outposts," Lieutenant Lyons explained. Then, addressing Marty, he continued, "Your squad will occupy this farmhouse. From the second floor you'll have a good view of the surrounding country. It's all fairly flat.

"All the outposts will keep in touch by using runners."

At last the fortunes of war had turned in our favor! We were moving into a house—a large, undamaged house! It seemed too good to be true, and when we entered the front door we met our first problem. The family who owned the house was still there. These people hadn't fled like the others in the area.

We had the usual problem of trying to communicate. No one was fluent in Italian and this family didn't speak English. Marty looked at me for help and once more my Latin was called upon to do the job. With great difficulty I became the interpreter.

I learned from the woman that she, her husband, and four children had remained at the farm because they had dairy cows and other livestock that needed care. On the first floor of the house was a large room that served as a living room, dining room and kitchen. There was also a bedroom. Upstairs were two more bedrooms.

"What are we going to do about them?" Scotty asked.

"I don't know," Marty answered. "What do you think we should do?"

Allen, the platoon medic, had chosen to stay with our squad, and he had the best suggestion.

"Why not let them stay downstairs and we'll take the upstairs bedrooms. Two rooms are enough for us and that way we'll have our observation post."

"O.K." Marty agreed. "Tell the Italians."

The woman seemed to understand me and quietly accepted the arrangement. She led us upstairs and also introduced her four children, two of whom were near our own ages.

Conquita, the oldest, was nineteen, Luciano was seventeen, and there were two younger children, a boy and a girl, who were under twelve years old.

Glad for a place to rest, we stayed in our rooms for the rest of the day, and the family remained downstairs. Outside it was so still that it seemed there was no war. From the glassless windows we could see for miles across quiet fields, grape vines and orchards.

On the first night it was my turn to sit by the window as a lookout. Everyone in the squad was sleeping and it was so dark outside that I could see nothing. The sky was covered with clouds that shut off the moonlight and stars.

The house was built of solid adobe covered with white plaster, and the window sills were a foot thick. The open windows could only be closed by pulling the heavy outside shutters together.

As I waited for the dark night to pass, my mind became suspicious and I began to fear for our safety. I became more nervous when, about ten o'clock, I heard a soft knock at the door and the man downstairs opened the latch. I heard a brief conversation in Italian by two men speaking in hushed voices. Then the visitor left and vanished into the night.

How did we know the man downstairs wasn't a fascist who would tip off the Germans? We could easily be trapped, for the stairway to my rear was the only way out.

The night had become very quiet and only the heavy breathing of our men disturbed the silence. It was a long, lonely watch.

In the early morning we went down to the well in the court-yard to wash our faces in the cold water. I shaved for the first time in several days. Suddenly we wanted to look neat and clean.

I had noticed that the brick floors and stairs of the farmhouse were uneven and badly worn. When I saw Conquita I asked her the age of the building. She smiled and told me it was over four hundred years old. That sounded like an eternity to me, and as I looked at the warped bricks of the stairs I could imagine many generations of walking feet. Fat baby feet that grew up to become old and wrinkled were constantly walking back and forth, wearing away the bricks.

The next night was very different from the first one. No sooner had darkness blotted out the haystack in the courtyard than footsteps clattered up the worn brick stairs. It had been prophesied by Daniels that we would not get another good night's sleep, but he was a pessimist and I would not accept such a reality. I would not miss my turn for a full night's sleep in a real bed.

However, Daniels, our new forty year old replacement, was right and the bad news had arrived with the messenger from our company. There would be another night of watching and waiting, only this time it would be out in the field.

Two men were to be left behind. We all wanted to be chosen, but Marty decided that Danels should stay because he had difficulty keeping up. Also, he snored loudly and we might be able to get some sleep in the field. Marty picked Davis as the other man to remain, but he gave no reason for his choice. However, the two men at the house were not to sleep. They, too, were to maintain a watch.

Again the night was very dark and in the blackness the ten of us stumbled our way across the stubble of a cornfield until we reached the path that followed along the edge of a large irrigation ditch. We were on top of a small levee beside a channel about four feet deep and fifteen feet across. A forest of tall bamboo grew down the middle of the ditch and the shrubbery was so thickly matted that we couldn't see the other bank.

Our mission for the night was to see if there was any enemy activity in the area, and we weren't sure how to proceed. There would be other American patrols out investigating other areas, but this particular sector was our squad's responsibility.

All the thick bamboo worried me. I didn't trust such places. It seemed the ditch beside the path would be an ideal place for the enemy to hide. When I mentioned this to Marty he decided we should take up such a position ourselves. We would lie in the ditch just beyond the bank and watch the path and the fields beyond. He placed two of us every thirty yards.

Ayers and I slipped over the grassy bank and made a hole in the dense shrubbery. Only our helmets were above the bank, and to our backs the bamboo was so thick that not even a light could shine through. It was doubtful if anyone could see us, yet, I felt uneasy because of the open field in front of us.

The corn had been harvested in the field and only the dry stocks remained. It seemed impossible to tell a person from a stock at night, so I stared hard to see if I could detect any movement. Along the left edge of the field were two rows of grape arbors about eight feet high. It was so dark under them that there could be a platoon of men and we couldn't see them.

Since we would be cut all night, we decided to take turns sleeping. I would watch for the first two hours while Ayers slept.

We had no jackets and the air was growing cold. The damp ground made me shiver. Above us the clouds were tearing apart allowing the bright stars to reach down and touch the earth, those same familiar points of light that made me think of peaceful nights at home.

Suddenly I was tense and alert! I heard something! A soft pounding! The muffled drum was growing louder and the beat was rapid. Someone was running. The pounding was growing very loud! A lot of feet were running! Behind us! On the other side of the bamboo! They were just a few feet away!

Ayers was awake. He heard it too and we looked at each other in silence. The bamboo was no shield against bullets and the slightest sound would alert the enemy patrol and we could expect to be raked with a machine pistol.

I stared at the heavy bamboo. It would be difficult for anyone to break through it. The footsteps were dying away, but I was thinking the patrol might return on our side of the channel. Then we would be faced with a decision. We only had our rifles, and Kraut patrols were armed with automatic weapons. If we opened fire we would have no way to escape. We couldn't pull back through the bamboo.

The grape arbor still looked menacing to me and I didn't want to get distracted. The wind was getting up, rustling the branches of the bamboo and making it difficult to hear other noises.

I was no longer sleepy, and Ayers was also sitting up, alert It was a long, cold night of waiting. There were streaks of gray in the sky before Marty came by whispering the orders to return to the farmhouse.

Each day we were becoming more friendly with our hosts. They were growing accustomed to our presence and their faces were less serious and tense, their actions more relaxed. My Latin continued to be our main way of communicating. Conquita insisted they did not speak Italian, but Tuscana. I knew little of dialects, but I found I could understand much of what they said.

Conquita, Luciano and their mother talked freely with me, but the father generally avoided us. He spent most of the time in the fields or doing farm chores. When we went through our morning ritual of washing and shaving by the well, Conquita came by and greeted us. Since she had red hair Truett called her "Capa rouge." When she smiled we all began to use that nickname.

Luciano sometimes came upstairs to talk with me. When I looked at his fair skin, blue eyes and curly blond hair I was reminded of the pictures of the Romans in my Latin book. From the window he pointed out the historic landmarks in Florence on the distant horizon. I told him he was lucky to be too young for the army and the war. The life of a soldier was not a good one.

We realized how the fear of us had vanished when the father came upstairs to where we were relaxing on the floor. With flashing eyes he held up a straight edge razor, pointing to the nicks in the blade. Evidently someone in our squad had used his razor for a tool for some purpose.

We all listened silently as he raved and scolded us with words we didn't understand. However, we all knew what he was saying. The razor must have been very valuable to him for him to confront us with such anger. I felt genuinely sorry that we had caused him this problem.

When he finished his speech he turned and stomped down the stairs. No one argued with him or showed any disrespect. We treated him as a father and when he was gone no one discussed the incident at all.

The mother had cut her hand while cooking in the kitchen and Allen, our medic, asked to see it. She was very skeptical and shook her head, but when I explained that he was our medic she reluctantly gave him her hand.

Allen carefully bandaged it and then noticed a sore place on her leg. She had skinned it and it had turned very red. After a close examination, Allen put medication and a bandage on this also.

With the treatment over, the mother and Conquita were smiling and relaxed. The ice had been broken and for the rest of the afternoon we all sat around in the kitchen visiting like old friends.

They asked me about the different men in the squad, pointing first to one and then another. I tried to give a little background about each one, but when I came to Ayers with his olive complexion I told them he was an Arab from Africa. Immediately they were very interested in him and Ayers wanted to know why they were staring.

When I told him, he didn't think it was funny and he became so angry he swore at me. I explained to our Italian hosts that I had been joking and that Ayers was really an American from Pennsylvania, but this didn't satisfy Ayers and he continued to scowl at me.

One morning a man who was a relative of the family came over to visit. I was in the courtyard when he arrived and he greeted me with all the warmth of a good friend, smiling and patting me on the back. He told me that the Americans and the Italians were of one heart, but not the Germans. He hated them and said all "Tedeschi" were bad. They carried off everything.

Later the mother repeated these same sentiments and I confused her by telling her that some Americans were of German decent, like our buddy, Rule. Then I tried to explain that the American army was made up of men of many nationalities, but this seemed to confuse her even more. Finally, to end the conversation I said that there were good people and bad people everywhere.

As we spent more time together the mother began to worry about our weapons and was afraid to have them near her. Since we never were without our rifles, always carrying them over our shoulders, we thought she would be more at ease if she understood more about them. We demonstrated how they were loaded and explained about the safety lock, but she only frowned and with her hands motioned for us to get them away.

Truett, always a lover, tried to get Luciano to arrange it so he could be alone with Conquita. Luciano didn't understand, or maybe he did. At any rate he became very nervous and turned pale. When he looked at me I told him in Latin to pay no attention to Truett.

Each evening after sunset our work began and our nightly patrols were continued. We roamed through our area and probed farther north looking for signs of enemy activity. One night we discovered another farmhouse and it was dark and appeared to be deserted. However, as we approached it we heard strange noises from inside. It seemed too dangerous for our small squad to investigate at night, so we circled around it and continued our patrol.

The weather was changing. Like animals we could sense it. Very soon booming thunder and lightning flashes started in the distance and began moving rapidly toward us. We were out in the open when the rain hit and it was like being in a shower with our clothes on. Without raincoats or jackets, we were instantly soaked. There was no shelter, no trees or buildings. We headed for the only thing around, a small wooden bridge that spanned a stream. We hoped to find some cover there, but the water was too high for us to squeeze under anywhere. As a last resort we climbed under some low bushes that grew along the bank of the creek and sat down in the mud to wait out the storm.

Our morale dropped rapidly in the wet and cold. How many times had we been miserable like that, and how many countless times in the future would we play the same scene? It seemed the war was a phonograph record stuck in a groove and we were doomed to a constant repetition of that night.

Marty was sitting beside me and he suddenly leaned over and laid his head in my lap. The sergeant image melted—his eyes were closed, he was a weary, lonely little boy.

I placed my hand on his shoulder, for his feelings were my own. How tired and deprived of all comforts we felt! How we hungered for affection!

As I looked down on him resting there I became aware of how his job as head of the squad had alienated him from the rest of us and made him even more lonely. He didn't move for a long time and neither of us said anything.

When the rain finally passed we all automatically got up and started the long walk back.

The following morning at the farm we were all excited by a news report that came over the company radio. The American army was in Aachen, Germany. We told the Italians "Americani in Allemagna" and "La guerra finito presto." The war would end soon!

We received some other news too. Trucks were waiting down the road to take us back for a rest.

Our Italian hosts watched solemnly as we filed out the door and I wondered what their thoughts were. Did they wonder how many of us would survive this continuing fight with the Germans? They knew they would not see us again.

As we walked down the road they waved goodby. I was sure they would be glad to get their rooms back, but I also felt they genuinely liked us.

Far from home while years go by
With a choice to fight or die.
Try to explain
A story that makes no sense,
It's self defense.
Our only time is now
It's endless.

"So your mother is English?" Clemens asks.

"Yes, I was just telling Jock, she's Scotch and English," I answer.

"Well, we may be related—if you go back far enough. How long since you've been home?"

"Less than a year. I had leave just before we shipped over."

"It's been five years for me," he shakes his head. "Can you imagine! Five years! First in Egypt and across Africa, and now here.

"Let me show you," he pulls out a wallet and flips it open. "Here's a picture of my sister. I just got it. She's eighteen. A beauty isn't she? When I left home she was thirteen. I don't even know her."

"Five years is a long time," I agree.

"And you know," Clemens continues, "you have something to go back to, but England is bombed and torn up. The factories are devastated. What have we got to look forward to?"

"We'll probably all be alcoholics," Jock adds.

"After the war a lot of things are going to be different," Everet says. "We have to give five years of our lives for the empire and all that's going to change. Sweden's got the right idea."

"There may not be another war for awhile," Clemens agrees. "This time everybody got bombed, not just the soldiers. Those buzz bombs don't care whose house they hit—rich man or poor man!"

"Let's have the show!" someone shouts.

"The show! The show!"

Four men climb up on the platform and begin to act out a skit on army life, but they are staggering and start shoving each other around. Three others join them and they all put their arms around one another's shoulders, holding each other up.

When they begin singing a burlesque song the audience joins in, but we don't know the words.

"Saturday night she takes it up the nose, down between the fingers, up between the toes"

"What time is it?" Ayers asks.

Marty has the watch, so we have to find him.

"After twelve," he shouts.

"We better get back," Denny suggests. "It's still the army and we have to get up in the morning."

"Come over again tomorrow night," Everet shouts. "We'll have more cognac—send somebody out for it every day."

We finally leave, shaking hands and vowing to continue the party.

EIGHT

We have been off the front for three days and it is as if we are reborn. Our animal instincts and survival impulses are still very keen and we have hair trigger reactions when there is a loud noise, but the summer sun is warm and suddenly life seems good.

It is still the army with morning calesthenics and daily hikes, but there is much free time. Some men are even lucky enough to get passes to go to town. Only a few are permitted to leave at one time, so the passes are given out by lottery. One man is chosen from each squad. In our squad we draw straws and Ayers is the lucky man.

When he leaves for town he plans to look for souveniers we can send home. No one has much money since we do not get paid regularly, but I give him the twenty dollars in occupation lira that I've been saving. I haven't yet sent anything to my parents and I don't know when I'll ever get a pass myself.

The rest of us are sitting in the sun writing letters or cleaning our weapons when a group of British soldiers walk through our area and disappear down into the nearby canyon. Soon others, both G.I.s and British, are cutting across the camp walking right past our tents and off toward the canyon. It has become a regular parade, and one in the group is Clemens.

"Hey," I call out to him, "where's everybody going?"

"Down in the ravine. A bunch of prostitutes came out from Florence. Everybody's going over."

"I'll be damned," Wallace says.

"There must be a hell of a lot of them, or a few are going to be awfully busy," I remark.

"God, they'll be rich," Martin adds.

"Is anybody here going?" Marty asks.

"Not with all those guys," Scotty shakes his head.

"Me either," Marty adds. "I like some privacy."

As more and more men trickle through, Pollack comes over and plops down beside me.

"Aren't any of you men going to join the crowd?" he asks.

"Hell no," Martin answers.

"I wouldn't mind," Pollack smiles. "I get the urge, but when I do I think of the wife and kid back home, so I sit down and write them a letter."

In the evening Ayers returns, but he doesn't have any souveniers. He gives back the money and says he didn't have time to look for anything. I don't question him and he doesn't offer any other explanation.

On our seventh day of rest there is big news. General Clark is going to make a speech to all the army men in Italy. He will speak in the evening on the radio-and we feel it must be something very important for he has not done this before.

There is also some excitement on our daily hike. Barnes finds a small puppy wandering around, so he takes him with us, buttoning him inside his shirt so only his head and ears are sticking out. This puts new spirit in everyone and all through the hike we are all calling out to the dog and suggesting names.

"We should have turns carrying him," Malik complains.

"Yes, we could make him a platoon mascot," Martin agrees.

At our evening chow we all save a little food for the puppy which causes Scotty to complain that we're over feeding him and we'll either make him sick or fat. Even with a full stomach the puppy is still running all around, so we pass the time playing with him while we wait for General Clark's speech.

When the time arrives we gather around the company radio to listen. Clark tells us that it is time for the final push to drive the Germans out of Italy. It is time to break the Gothic line and clear the Po valley before winter. This will deprive the Germans of the industrial supplies they are getting from the Po.

The final news is a real shock and shatters our morale. We are all stunned! Our division is being committed. We will be moving into the line, replacing the Eighty-fifth who relieved us just a week ago. After all of our high hopes for a long rest, we have been in army reserve for only a week.

We are reeling from the sudden, unexpected and complete change of fortune. There will be no sleep tonight, for the order has already come to prepare to move out. We will be leaving before it is dark. To add to our sinking morale the sky is clouding over and rain appears imminent.

"It's going to be cold up there in the Appenines," Ayers says. "Maybe we should carry blankets."

"That would be too much trouble in combat," I object. "I want to be able to run. A blanket will slow you down and get in the way."

"How about a half of a blanket? I'll cut one down the middle and we can each carry half. Then at night we can put the two halves together and wrap up in them."

Ayers quickly splits the blanket and rolls one half up, tying it with a rope that can be looped over his shoulder. Seeing his eagerness I finally agree and roll up the other half.

Marty comes over scowling, ready to explode.

"You know what that screwed up supply outfit has done? Our PX ration just arrived. Here we're ready to leave and they send us cases of beer for a beer party!"

"Those bastards," Ayers agrees. "Doesn't anyone know what's going on. The officers won't let us have any beer now."

While we are dividing up the candy bars and looking through the paper back books that came in with the ration, Everet stops in to see what we're doing.

"I just came over to arrange a trade with your cooks, some of our bully beef for that spam you all hate--but, what's going on? It looks like everyone's packing up."

"Remember that Gothic line?" Marty asks. "Well, we're not going to miss it after all. We just got our orders."

"I'm damned sorry to hear this," Everet says.

"So are we," Wallace agrees.

"We've been planning a good party for tonight. We're going to miss you Yanks."

"Well, have a few drinks for me," Ayers says. "In fact you can have my beer."

This sounds like such a great idea that we give all of our PX beer to the British. We feel we owe them some liquor anyhow.

The trucks and a light rain arrive at the same time. Climbing into the open truck beds, we drape blankets over us and huddle together. No one talks as we bounce along the ruts in the road. When, in the past, we have passed British soldiers riding up to the front they were all singing, but the Americans are always silent.

I am thinking of a recent conversation we all had in which many of my buddies expressed a fear of being killed just as the war was ending. After having gone through so much suffering and peril, and with the end of the war in sight, no one wanted to be the last casualty. Yet, as I look at the bodies huddled around me, I know that some will not come back this time.

NINE

It is late at night and we have finally made contact with the Eighty-fifth division. The trucks carried us as far as they dared and it was still light when we began traveling in our usual way, single file with our rifles at sling arms.

We saw General Clark's jeep at a dusty intersection. He was standing up, waving to the troops and urging us on, but we did not share his enthusiasm.

After that there were hours of climbing into the foothills where it was so dark that we could hardly see the trail and shrubs around us.

It is a ghostly scene as we pass through the Eighty-fifth. We are walking by shadowy figures moving among the trees and they are faceless in the dark night.

"Can't you bastards fight?"

"Did you rest so long you got soft?"

Derisive comments cut through the night. They are our army brothers, but we are angry and disappointed with no way to vent our frustrations and unable to understand the logic of the gererals

We leave these silent men of the Eighty-fifth to fade like phantoms, disappearing to the rear. We walk on through the night with no thoughts of sleep and with no contact with the enemy.

The fading night and growing light of dawn gradually reveals the rugged mountain country. Tall peaks and green slopes covered with large pines come into sharp focus. In the distance we can see green meadows and farm buildings cradled among the giant rocks and trees. A tiny strip of gray ribbon, far below us, winds through a narrow valley among the steep mountains. It is an umbilical cord between Florence and the Po valley to the North, a vital corridor to both sides in this war.

Suddenly the valley below becomes alive with fighting. We are gods on Mt. Olympus looking down on a war between mortals. Tiny tanks are moving slowly forward and puffs of white smoke mark exploding shells. Toy soldiers are running among the trees and shrubs. The sounds of machine gun and rifle fire seem strangely distant.

The Americans are slowly beating their way through the pass and our role becomes clear. We are to secure this high ridge on the western flank.

Advancing once more we follow the foot path that leads along the side of the mountain. A machine gun opens up! Bullets thump the earth around us! Everyone leaps for cover!

The gun is firing at close range from among some rocks and the closest cover is a small stone building without a door. I dive through the doorway and find Martin and Lieutenant Lyons inside. The machine gun rakes the doorway sending a row of bullets spinning across the dirt floor.

Instinctively we examine the room for another way out. It is a small one room building with a window in the back. The window is high above the dirt floor, at least seven feet to the sill, and there is no glass so it is open to the sky.

"Stay away from the door!" Martin says. "Should we try to go out the window?" I ask.

"No," Lieutenant Lyons says. "We don't know what's out there."

Martin shakes his head and keeps both eyes on the door.

Both Lieutenant Lyons and Martin think we should wait a few minutes and then dash out the door. This seems suicidal to me.

"We'll dash out and hit the dirt," Lieutenant Lyons says. "Now!"

The three of us make a mighty leap through the doorway and roll to the ground. There is only silence. Martin jumps up and runs over toward the path. Still silence. Lieutenant Lyons and I join him and we find the rest of our company spread out on the ground along the path.

Suddenly we hear the Kraut machine gun again. It is firing in the window of the stone building. They have moved the gun around to the back of the building!

While the rest of our company advances along the path, a squad is sent back to hunt for the Jerry machine gun. One man in the platoon has to be carried. During the initial machine gun attack he was hit in both legs.

Denny signals for the company to stop and the wounded man is stretched out on the path. I see that it is Barnes and he is in great pain.

"We need to get some medics to carry Barnes to an aid station," Denny says. "Someone will have to go down into the pass and try to contact the companies down there and ask them for some medics. Will anyone volunteer to go?"

There are no voices and no hands. Everyone stands silently. I look at Barnes and I look at all the silent faces. Barnes came over seas with me.

"I'll go," I tell Denny.

He looks at me and nods solemnly. "Try to stay under cover. We need four medics and a litter."

I have put myself in the situation I fear most. I am alone at the front and don't know where the enemy is hiding. I start down through the brush with all my instincts for survival aroused. Every rock and every tree could hide an enemy. I try to look everywhere at once, but all I see is dense brush and chaparral. I think that speed will give me an element of surprise if I should stumble onto a Kraut, so I try running down the steep slope.

As I near the valley I have another fear. The Americans might mistake me for a Kraut and open fire. Slowing down, I cautiously approach a dirt road that runs along the edge of the pass. It looks deserted, but well traveled, covered with dusty footprints.

Lying down behind the shrubs at the side of the road, I decide to wait for someone to pass. Within minutes a large group of men, at least a platoon, comes into view. They draw near and I can see that they are G.I.s. How to contact them without startling anyone?

There are more men following them--at least a company. Everyone is moving south. Are they withdrawing? When they are right in front of me I call out.

"Medic! I need a medic!"

Instantly the entire company stops and an officer walks toward me. I sit up and hold up my hand. Then I slowly rise to my feet.

When I tell the lieutenant about our wounded man he immediately calls for four medics to go with me. He also tells me that the Americans are temporarily pulling back.

As the four medics and I start back up the mountain, I am more nervous than ever. They do not try to stay under the cover of the chaparral, but walk right out in the.open relying on their white helmets with the red crosses to protect them. I think the Germans will probably respect those white helmets shining in the sunlight, but I do not have such an insignia. A sniper with a telescopic sight could easily pick me out.

It is a long, slow climb, but finally we reach the company area. Barnes is still lying quietly on the path and he shows no emotion as the medics quickly check his wounds. The litter is unfolded and placed on the ground next to the injured man.

The four medics gently push him onto the litter. He is a big man and it will be a rough trip down through the brush. There is no time to lose. They will have to rush to catch up with the withdrawing column.

The company has been waiting for my return, and after the medics and Barnes disappear into the shrubbery the order is given to advance once more. Captain Mathews is very concerned about my report that the companies in the valley are withdrawing, and he fears we may be left isolated out in front of the rest of the troops.

We move slowly now, searching the area carefully but staying together near the path, probing blindly with no information about enemy strengths or positions. We do not know that we are tired. All awareness is concentrated on survival.

It grows dark and Captain Mathews gives an order for us to all lie down on the path and remain completely silent. We are not to dig in for that would make a noise. The dark is our cloak of security.

Two man outposts are to be set up all around the company and the rest of us are to take turns staying awake. Half of the company is to remain awake at all times. Ayers and I will trade off, one hour of sleep and one hour awake.

Even when it is my turn to sleep I can't relax. The night is filled with strange noises and I can see nothing in the total darkness. The heavy clouds allow no light at all from the moon or stars. The hours pass and I remain wide awake.

It is almost morning, but still dark, when our northern outpost hears men coming along the path. The unknown patrol is ordered to hault and challenged to be recognized.

They can't see each other and are just voices in the night. Our outpost doesn't ask for the password for the night since we have not received one. It is never a reliable indication of friend or foe anyhow. Axis Sally usually broadcasts it on the radio every evening about six o'clock, before we have even received it from the rear.

The leader of the patrol, speaking perfect English, says they are Americans and asks permission to pass through.

The outpost doesn't answer. There's no room for error. The stakes are high—the survival of the company.

The patrol leader again asks for permission to pass.

Finally the man on outpost answers.

"In New York we have the Yankees. What's the ball club in Chicago?

There's no answer.

"What's the club in Detroit?"

There is only silence.

"Doesn't anybody in your patrol know?"

More silence. The patrol has withdrawn.

TEN

The world we have entered is not part of this century. Climbing single file high into the mountains we wound along a narrow trail that led us through a pass and into this isolated valley. Below us is a picture from a medieval painting. We are in a time warp, in an ancient world where there are no Germans and there is no war.

It is not so much a valley as a deep ravine with a river far below. Rocky terraces scale the steep slopes on both sides. Ancient hands have dug out the terraces and built the rock retaining walls that climb like steps up the mountains and hold the narrow shelves of soil, protecting it from the erosion of the Appenine snows.

The grape vines and corn that is growing on the terraces is stunted and sickly looking. The poor soil and harsh climate take their toll.

The river below has crystal clear water that sparkles in the sunlight as it follows a twisting path, snaking among the mountains A stone bridge spans the river and next to it are a cluster of low stone buildings with slate roofs. I have seen such pictures in old Roman engravings. There is no sign of life and the absolute silence suggests sorcery.

Denny passes the word that the company is going to stop for lunch, so we spread out along the terraces and sit on the rock walls with our feet dangling.

I draw a ration from inside my shirt, rip open the box and taste the biscuit. As usual no one is talking and we observe quietly and think our own thoughts.

The spell is broken when some children come out of a house below and a boy begins to climb up the terraces toward us. He ambles over the rocks like a mountain goat, and I judge him to be about twelve. As he approaches he waves and shouts.

"Buona Giorno!"

"Buona Giorno. Buona Giorno," we reply.

We try English with him, but he doesn't understand, and he tries Italian with us, but we have difficulty communicating. With my limited vocabulary I ask him where the Germans are and he says he hasn't seen any. This I understand.

Ayers holds up his canteen and points to the river. The boy grins and takes the canteen. Immediately Marty and Martin hand him their canteens to fill. The other two children join us and they take more canteens and run down to the river after the boy. When they all return with the cool water we thank them and give them gum or candy from our rations.

As I look at the narrow strips of farm land I wonder if the farmers plow them with the white oxen they use in other parts of Italy. It is a marvel that anyone can support a family in such a harsh environment. The children are smiling and look healthy and I am thinking that as difficult as the life is here these people are better off in this isolated environment than are many of their countrymen in this war torn country. In fact, removed from the world they are better off than we are at the present time.

We stay for only an hour and as we leave the children stand waving after us. This remote setting has given me something to think about as I walk wearily along the rough trail. I wonder how life would be in such a place where the only contact with Florence or the Po valley is by way of the rough trail we are following, a trail used mainly by the mule trains that carry charcoal out of the mountains to be used for fuel in the valleys.

In my mind I can see the women carrying baskets of clothing on their heads down to the stream to do the washing, and I imagine them using wooden churns to turn the goat's milk into butter and cheese. In the winter when the stream is frozen over and snow covers the slate roofs the families would sit around the stone fireplaces trying to keep warm.

It is a simple life. Yet, I envy them when I think what lies ahead of us.

In future days those children can tell of the time the American soldiers passed through. It was a brief encounter between two different worlds.

It is hard to shake the feeling that we have dropped back in time. The trail is a twisting, circling maze that climbs and decends, crosses streams and turns around giant boulders. It is impossible to keep a sense of direction, and the only signs of human activities are the large round cleared areas that we occasionally run across. These are black from burning charcoal.

Everyone is alert, but the tension is missing. There is no feeling of war. Are we hypnotized by the isolation of the mountains? Can we no longer sense danger?

All at once we see them! Footprints in the dusty path— footprints with hob nailed soles. The Krauts have been here!

Our column spreads out and scouts are sent ahead. There is a stone building right beside the path. The Krauts like houses!

The door of the house flies open and a group of Italians rush out waving and shouting, "Tedeschi tutti via!"

They are screaming that the Germans have gone. They rush up smiling and laughing, grabbing the scouts and hugging them. Captain Mathews and Lieutenant Lyons talk with them and they explain that they are partizans and work with the Italian underground. They tell us that the Germans saw us coming and fled leaving their half finished meals on the table. They had not expected us so soon.

One of the partizans has exciting news for us. They have been hiding eleven American and British pilots in a nearby cave. When these pilots were shot down over the Po valley the partizans rescued them and hid them until they could be brought into the mountains and taken to the cave.

While we wait at the house one of the partizans slips away to bring the missing pilots back to us. Within an hour he returns with the grinning airmen who are happier to see us than the partizans were. Some have been hiding in the cave for over nine months. The partizans have been smuggling food to them.

After sharing our rations with these men, who can hardly believe they've been rescued, Captain Mathews assigns a patrol to escort them back to the rear. The rest of the company continues to pursue the fleeing Germans.

ELEVEN

We are a string of elephants as we advance through the mountains at night. Each man has a firm grasp on the shoulder of the man ahead of him, for he can't see him as he stumbles along blindly.

In the absolute darkness the rough path is treacherous. A sudden bend in the trail throws me off balance and sends me crashing into some brush and when the man ahead of me trips he drags me down with him. All night it is the blind leading the blind. We can only trust that somewhere up the line someone knows where we are going and can find our objective.

The word comes from the back of the line, "lost contact in the rear." The line comes to a hault and we all stand in silence waiting for the last man to go back and find the man that should be behind him. At last the word comes that contact has been established and the column moves forward again.

On and on we go until, from some anonymous being at the head of the line, the word comes to stop and dig in. Marty designates a squad area and Ayers and I dig another slit trench.

I carry a shelter half folded over my belt and when there is rain we stretch it over our hole. To do this we must dig deep enough so that our heads are below ground level when we are sitting up. Of course with the cover on we can't see out and that can be dangerous.

For the rest of the night the men in the squad take turns
staying awake and watching. We have one watch with a luminous dial and this is passed from slit trench to slit trench every two hours.

It seems that I am no sooner asleep than someone is shaking me and handing me the watch. I arouse Ayers and the two of us sit peering into the darkness, listening to all the strange sounds of the night. Two hours is an eternity. It seems impossible to stay awake and we are not sure if we are dozing or dreaming. At such times it is hard to distinguish between imagination and reality.

Finally it is again my time to get some sleep and I crawl over to Scotty's hole and slip him the watch.

I awake with a start. People are shouting and firing guns. By the early morning light I get my first view of the surrounding country. We are on the slope of a mountain covered with all shades of green. There are patches of grass mixed with many small bushes, tall pines and huge granite boulders. Everything is dripping from the light drizzle. The fog hangs in little puffs like smoke among the trees. We are on a cloudy peak and the action around us is something from mythology.

Small men, clad in green garmets and wearing Robin Hood hats are racing around yelling and firing shots.

"Italian alpine troops," Ayers says. "They've trapped a mountain goat and plan to have a meal."

I have seen these men before when they led the mule trains that bring our supplies into the mountains. We were told that before the war they trained in these mountains and learned to live off the land. Watching them leaping and yelling is like watching boys playing an exciting game. I never see the goat, and soon the men disappear among the rocks.

It feels good to climb out of the trench and stretch my stiff legs, and already our company is preparing to move on.

We are on a trail that is as wide as a California logging road. On one side the mountain rises steeply, covered with a heavy forest. On the other side it drops off abruptly to form a deep gorge with a river below.

Since the trail follows the river gorge I can see the tumbling water with its rapids and waterfalls. The scenery is magnificent, and the morning sun filters down through the branches above to form shadowy patterns on the dirt road.

Suddenly I see that there is more than dead wood and leaves along the trail. A human leg with a German boot is lying there. Other pieces of human bodies are scattered all along the road. The sight is grotesque and sickening and I open and close my eyes to be sure that what I am seeing is real.

The artillery must have scored a direct hit on a group of German soldiers blowing them to bits. The sobering sight blots out the beauty. The magic is gone.

The trail turns away from the river and abruptly starts down into another ravine. It goes down, across a tiny stream that we can easily jump over, and angles up the other side.

"At last we get to go down," Marty says. "Of course we'll have to climb the other side."

Before anyone else can comment, a machine gun opens fire and Kraut bullets kick up the dirt at the bottom of the ravine. Like rabbits we scatter and hit the ground.

While the gun continues to fire, Captain Mathews, Lieutenant Lyons and Denny huddle together and study the situation. Denny tells us the decision.

"The Kraut guns don't have the range to hit us here, but they can cover the bottom of the ravine. By the angle of fire it looks like the trail on the other side is under them, so if we get across the bottom we should be able to move up the trail safely.

"See, down in the bottom of the ravine there is a fallen log," he points. "That should give cover. So, one man at a time we'll run down the trail, hurdle the log and drop down behind it. The Kraut gun will be firing at the man running down the trail, so when the next man starts down, the one behind the log will get up and run on up the other side."

The advance begins. One by one the men in the company race down to the log, and each time a man runs the Kraut machine gun fires.

It is my turn to go, and with my heart pounding in my throat I run faster than I have ever run in my life. It is down hill, but it is a long ways. I am zig-zagging with my eyes glued on the log, terrified by the rattling of the machine gun.

With a long jump I hurtle the fallen tree and land on top of a man lying on the other side.

"You were supposed to take off when I started down," I tell him

"I can't run," he answers. "I hurt my leg when I went over the log. I can't stand on it."

The next man is starting down the hill and there is not room for anyone else behind the log, so I leave the injured man and run to the other side.

The trail up is steep, but I fear the Krauts may move their machine gun or bring up reinforcements, so I continue to run until my chest hurts and my legs ache.

Where the trail levels off again the others are waiting, and as I reach them I find it is drizzling on this side of the mountain. Denny and Lieutenant Lyons are sitting on a large boulder with an army blanket draped over their heads and around their shoulders trying to keep dry. The tall trees don't offer much shelter from the rain.

We are talking quietly, feeling a sense of relief after crossing the ravine safely when we are deafened by a series of thundering explosions. I dive for the ground ! Artillery!

"Medics!" Denny yells.

What has happened to Lieutenant Lyons? Denny is laying him down on the road. He has collapsed unconscious and has a strange color in his face.

Allen comes running and quickly rips the lieutenant's shirt off. We gather around staring, knowing that it is hopeless. His body is riddled with shrapnel. He is bleeding from a dozen places in the chest. He is dead. Popular, handsome Lieutenant Lyons is dead. Lieutenant Lyons who always had a joke for us is dead.

What about Denny who was huddled with him when the shell hit?

He is untouched! Unhurt as he was a month before when a sniper put a bullet between the eyes of the man next to him. As he was when the man on either side of him was killed by an air burst. He has a shield around him! He walks out in the open directing an attack and remains untouched.

What is the pattern? Why the protection? Why are some men killed on the first day of combat?

The company is all together again and we advance looking for the machine gun, but we don't find it. We move on until evening when we come to some abandoned houses.

While we stop to eat our rations Denny tells us that the man who was injured by the log has a broken leg. The medics have carried him back to an aid station.

"A million dollar injury," Malik says.

"A ticket home," Wallace agrees. "It takes too long for a broken leg to heal. They need the hospital beds over here so they'll ship him home."

"We'd all be better off if we broke our legs," someone said. "That guy was lucky!"

"Luckier than Lieutenant Lyons!"

For many days the fighting is continuous. We are striking farther into the mountains and reaching the fortified positions of the Gothic line. The Germans fall back from one prepared position to another always looking down on us from the heights. Again we lead an animal existence, not thinking, but hunting and reacting.

The war goes on with a steady attrition. One day someone is killed, the next day two or three, and on good days only a few are wounded or injured. These men from our company are usually unknown to us, nameless replacements. Yet, our squad is still without any serious casualties.

It is hard to understand how we can continue to do our jobs day after day when we are always tired, wet and cold, but such things do not enter our consciousness. These things are suppressed. We know we are miserable, but our main conscious awareness is devoted to what is going on around us. We are listening, watching, smelling. Alert! Alert!

We aren't really homesick either. We don't think much about anything, for nothing can be allowed to interfere with our keen attention.

Being in the mountains and the farm valleys we are always vulnerable. We feel it, walking in the open and advancing. We rarely see the enemy, but we are shot at, shelled, bombed with mortar shells, hit with machine gun fire from the buildings and high places, worried about mine fields and booby traps.

Without much sleep we are still alert, animal alert, not realizing we are tired and never sleeping deeply when the opportunity comes.

On and on, doing what is expected of us, not thinking of the killed or wounded. Shutting it all from our minds, knowing that any second we could be the same. We seal our minds from all the carnage to protect our sanity. We have learned to make the screen blank.

Besides the dangers all around us we have to give attention to the simple necessities of life. We have to have rations, to find water and to maintain body functions. Elimination is a special problem since we often have diarhea. We risk dangers crawling away from our slit trenches to not foul our beds. It is a nervous experience just to take our pants down and we do things as quickly as possible. The intestinal problems may come from drinking water from many sources. Fortunately there is always toilet paper in the rations.

After a long day of marching through the rugged mountains it is my turn to find water and fill the canteens. My buddies and I have worked out an arrangement so we will not all have to hike down to some stream every night.

With one canteen hooked over each finger, holding each by the chain that connects the cap, I ramble off in search of water. Skidding and jumping down the steep slope of a canyon I hunt around until I find a small stream.

As I start the climb back with the full canteens, the chains cut into my fingers and not being able to use my hands to grab the rocks and shrubs, it is a tortuous climb toward the ridge. Finally, after much slipping and stumbling, the company is in sight.

When I stop to catch my breath my foot slips on a rolling rock. Jerking to catch myself, I see two canteens jump from my fingers and take off down the mountain like boulders in an avalanche.

I am lucky! They don't go too far, but lodge against some bushes. I retrieve the first one, but as I reach for the second it skips away and plunges into the darkness below.

My tired back and legs cry out for rest and my mind says "to hell with it," but I know I can't go back without it. Water is more precious than gold. We ration ourselves carefully, and every man must have a canteen.

Below it is a dark cave and to find the canteen among the brush and rocks seems impossible. I retrace the steps I took, searching in vain. Deeper down the slope I go and my morale drops to zero as I fear I may never find the vagrant. Without it I will have to give up my own canteen, so I must continue the search.

Like a miracle the starlight touches the aluminum just enough for me to see a spot of silver nestled in a bush. With all the canteens on my fingers again I struggle up to the summit.

TWELVE

Like a ghostly illusion in the moonlight the pale bridge sculpured from sandstone connects the two hills. Devoid of all vegetation, it shines like a streak of light on a black canvas.

We are gathered together on the the dark hill looking at the strange road that leads across to our objective, a hill that glows in the night like a misty cloud. To cross over will be like following a footbridge across a river, and we don't like it.

"It's too open," Marty says. "We'll have to go single file and there's no room to maneuver."

"It's like being in a spotlight," Ayers agrees.

"In this moonlight we might as well be crossing in daylight," Martin adds.

We can already see the advance platoon of the company starting across the bridge and the dark uniforms make the men clearly visible against the light surface. I shudder when I see it, for there is nothing an infantry man hates worse than being out in the open with no cover.

We are starting to move, the last part of that dark centipede that is crawling across the light bridge. Since our squad is toward the end of the line I feel sure the Krauts will have our company spotted before we reach the bridge and we will get there just in time to catch hell from the mortars and artillery.

As we walk out onto the bridge I am close behind Marty and Wallace. I want to run, but can go no faster than the men ahead of me. On either side of us there is a brush covered ravine that looks black in contrast to the moonlit sandstone. We are on a stage and I feel there is an audience in those black pits. The bridge seems a natural place for the Krauts to make a defense, but the night is strangely silent. Are they waiting for us all to be on the bridge before they strike?

I am a fourth of the way across, half way across—then I see something gleaming in the bushes. The barrel of a machine gun! Before I can react I see the rest of the picture. Beside the gun sprawls the body of a dead Kraut. The advance patrol did its job.

Safely across, the company is spreading out on the gray colored hill. WHOOM! Fire is dancing from the rocks, the ground is heaving and concussions slap my ears.

I hug the ground with no protection as the barrage continues. Frantically trying to dig while lying on my stomach, I bang the shovel into the ground, but all I hit is rock.

The shrapnel is whirring and clanging off the boulders! Ayers, Rule and I team up, working on our knees, desperately trying to dig out the rocks, but they are too large for the three of us to dislodge. The shrapnel is whining and screaming as we wildly try one spot after another.

There are yells and calls for medics, but no let up in the shelling.

"Build sangars!" a voice says. "We were in a spot like this before and we had to pile up the rock around us."

Desperately, with our hands, we scratch for rock, trying to build up a cockpit. Many of the rocks are in slabs and won't budge.

"Whoosh-boom! There is a new sound in the night. I recognize it instantly, the sound of a German 88 mm. cannon. A tank has pulled up just below the hill and is firing directly into our positions.

"To the other side of the hill!" Denny yells.

Afraid to raise up, but more afraid to stay put we crawl and stumble through the shell fire to escape the tank. The other side of the hill gives us cover from the tank, but the artillery shells are raining down and the ground here is covered with rock also.

Ayers and I both spot some huge boulders overhanging the ravine. They are as big as houses and if we can get under them they will provide a temporary shelter from the shrapnel that is ricochetting from rock to rock.

It is a good choice! A cave as large as a room cuts back under the boulders and more than a dozen men from the company are already there. Captain Mathews and Denny are there too, along with Lieutenant James and another sergeant. Captain Mathews is holding a map and talking seriously with the others.

There is a loud bang on the boulder above our heads and we see a shell drop down in front of us and crash into the ravine below.

"A dud," Ayers says.

"What if it hadn't been?" I ask. "If it had gone off would it have dislodged this boulder? We could be buried here!"

Captain Mathews is still talking earnestly. He didn't even look up when the dud hit.

The shelling has become sporadic, so Ayers and I agree it is safer to get out from under the boulder and go out on the hill. We start gathering rock and soon have a two foot wall built up around us.

"Thud!" All our rocks are rattling. Another dud has landed, and this one hit right beside us. Ayers and I are flat in our shallow bed trembling and praying silently.

The shelling completely stops and as clouds drift across the moon a light rain starts to fall. We spread the shelter half over the rocks, but there is to be no sleep.

"Did you hear that?" Ayers asks.

"Yes," I answer, for I too hear a strange crying in the night

From the black ravine below the boulders a voice cries out several times. It is an agonized cry for help.

Is it a G.I.? A Kraut? A trick of some kind? We listen silently as the cry is repeated. It sounds pathetic, yet fearful and terrified.

Three men from the company are planning to go down into the darkness to investigate. The next thing we hear is Denny's voice calling out.

"There's a wounded Kraut down there in a house. He can't walk—been hit in the leg. Are there any volunteers to carry him back to the aid station? I won't ask anyone to do it, after what's been happening here."

It will take four men to carry him on a litter and there are three volunteers. They are standing waiting. Abruptly I agree to be the fourth man. I am dead tired, but I can't leave a suffering man. Any of us could be as he is.

The house with the wounded Kraut has been a supply point. There are cases of sardines and other food from Bologna. They are a tempting change from our K rations, but we are afraid to touch anything, fearful of booby traps.

It is hard carrying the man up out of the ravine. He is very heavy and it is too dark to see the trail. We constantly stumble and fall through the bushes.

We don't know how far it is to the aid station and every step is difficult because the rain has made the path slippery. One of us is constantly falling and jerking. Every time we jolt the litter the Kraut moans. He does not speak English so we can't communicate, but occasionally he asks in Italian, "Quanta kilometer?"

"Uno," I keep answering, although I have no idea how far we have come or how much farther we have to go to reach the aid station. We're not even sure we are going the right way. It would be easy to get turned around in the dark and none of us have been this way before. Finally, we meet a medic on the path and he gives us final directions--we are almost there.

When we are used to no lights at all it is surprising how comforting the soft glow of candles can be. The small room looks peaceful and secure. Two medics are quietly putting bandages on two wounded G.I.s.

We place the litter on the floor and one of the medics immediately gives the same attention to the injured Kraut that he has been giving to the hurt Americans.

Our reward is being allowed to spend the few remaining hours of the night in the hay in the stable. I am tired, but I feel satisfied. We spend all of our days and nights hunting and killing, and for the first time in a long time I have done something humane. I have a need for this. The fact that this man is a Kraut doesn't matter, although many of my buddies don't feel this way.

With the first light of dawn we are on the muddy trail again. I don't know any of the others who helped carry the Kraut, but they are from my company, and we know we will be expected back.

When we arrive back at the drab, barren hill we find all the rock dugouts deserted. The entire company is gone.

"Hey!" a voice calls out. A solitary figure is ambling toward us. "I'm supposed to meet you and lead you to the company."

Before our guide has taken more than a few steps he slips on the rocks and injures his ankle so severely that we have to take him back to the aid station.

Now we are growing anxious. How do we find the company when it is advancing? If we miss it we could get ahead of the line and wander into Kraut territory.

As we leave the aid station a mule train is arriving. The animals are loaded with cartons of rations and medical supplies. They are not handled by Italians, but rather three G.I.s are leading them along the muddy trail. In the steady drizzle the men and mules look like gray shadows plodding along heedless of the weather or the war. They are as mindless ghosts condemned to eternally lug their burdens over muddy mountain trails.

When we question the leader of the pack train he tells us he has supplies for our battalion, and when we ask to accompany him he welcomes us, glad to have some riflemen along. The Krauts often infiltrate to attack the supply trains.

The trail is a brutal one with dead Germans and Kraut equipment scattered all along the way. In the mud and the rain the barbaric scene is especially depressing. Where is the glory? We see only degredation.

After a few miles the men with the supplies think they have gone far enough, so we leave them and search ahead for our company. It is late in the afternoon when we find some of the men clustered by a group of houses.

Some small caves have been discovered in the hills behind the houses and Captain Mathews, seeing that everyone is desperately tired, thinks this will be a good place to spend the night. It would be too dangerous to stay in the houses. The Krauts are sure to shell them.

Joining Ayers once more, I search for a cave where we can rest. We agree on a hole that has been dug back into the hill. Although it is raining hard, the hole is dry inside. Since it is not big enough for us to lie down, Ayers sits at one end and I am at the other. Our legs are stretched out in front of us, but because of the narrow quarters our feet are practically in each other's lap.

About midnight the water begins seeping down through the dirt roof to form an icy pool on the floor. Chunks of mud also begin to drop from the ceiling and soon the entire floor is a large pool of icy mud.

"Don't move and we'll stay warm," Ayers tells me.

I am shivering, my feet are cold and my legs ache. I have to shift my body and bend my stiff legs, but every time I move Ayers swears at me. It is a cold, miserable, muddy, sleepless night for us both and it seems it will never pass. We are suffering eternally in a cold hell.

THIRTEEN

It is more like a dream than reality, a dream with no ending and no logic. In absolute darkness, my only link with the human world is the touch of my hand on Marty's shoulder ahead of me and the feel of Ayers fingers tugging at the collar of my shirt from behind.

We are stumbling up a trail that we can't see toward another objective whose existance we accept on faith. Krauts are en-trenched on the ridge ahead.

I'm determined not to lose my grip on Marty's shoulder, although we are both stumbling, but without warning I'm jerked off balance and there is a crashing sound with the clatter of equipment up ahead.

"The guy in front of me went to sleep," Marty says.

When the line starts moving again I crash into some bushes that scratch at my helmet and pull at my equipment.

"Lost contact in the rear," Ayers passes the word.

Again the line stops until we hear the break in the line has been repaired and contact has been established.

The night comes alive with the rattle of two Kraut machine guns. Tracers, like fiery rockets, are spraying out from the ridge seeking unseen targets. They have the beauty of fireworks, like hot cinders that burn out before they reach us. We are beyond the range of the deadly shower.

We continue like a line of cardboard soldiers moving forward with conditioned reflexes, pressed together into a giant worm that is inching its way up the mountain. More Kraut machine guns join the action. The Krauts sense our nearness.

The sounds are coming from many places and some of the guns are not firing tracers. It seems impossible to get through this heavy brush that we can't see and attack those guns that can be anywhere in the blackness.

How can we keep in contact with each other when the fighting starts? How can we keep from shooting each other?

Evidently others have been thinking the same thoughts, for Marty passes back an order to reverse direction. We will fall back to the last ridge and call for the artillery to pound the Krauts. Then we will attack at dawn.

Going down is not much easier. We slip and tumble into each other until we reach the bottom of the ravine. After that we are struggling up once again.

There is so much brush on the top of the ridge that it is hard to find a place to dig. Ayers and I attack the hard, rocky soil and work our way down about two feet. There we hit a large rock that we can't dig out. Finally, using a piece of a tree limb for a lever we are able to budge it, but when we pry it out of the hole our success is a disaster.

Water is flowing through the bottom of the slit trench. The rock was damming an underground spring. The underground stream is now flowing in one end and out the other.

"Where the hell's the water going? The trench isn't filling up." Ayers is on his knees with his head down in the hole.

"We cut one of the earth's arteries," I tell him.

Desperately we try to wedge the rock back into the hole, but it's like trying to put back an extracted tooth. The genie once free won't be contained again.

To add to our water problems a rain is beginning to fall.

"Maybe that artery leads right down to the sea and this whole damn country will sink," Ayers says.

"That's alright with me," I agree, "but right now the Krauts are on the next ridge and it isn't safe to be above ground."

"Well it's too damn late to try to dig another hole in this ground," Ayers throws down his shovel.

I start doing the only thing I can think of, cutting some brush and piling it in the bottom of the slit trench. Since the flowing water is only six inches deep we can lay a shelter half on top of the branches and climb in on top of it.

The rain has stopped again and the clouds are breaking up. Stretching out at last, I search the sky for stars and listen to the whistling of the artillery shells passing over. Then I am amazed at the most spectacular display of shell fire I have seen in the war. The next ridge is ablaze with huge fountains of fire. Sparklets are lighting up everywhere.

"It's white phosphorus," Denny says. "I'd hate to be the Krauts. When that stuff hits you it'll burn right into your skin. Nothing will put it out. It'll burn under water."

We listen to the booms of the exploding shells, and each one sends a shower of fiery particles in all directions.

I do not sleep at all, watching and wondering what the dawn will bring. With the first streaks in the eastern sky the order comes to advance again.

We follow the same trail, only this time it is light enough to make out the faint outlines of the bushes and rocks. We again climb up toward the ridge, but no machine guns are firing. Are the Krauts lying in wait?

We continue single file until we reach the summit. Then spreading out we cross over the last hill and continue walking across a level plateau. There are slit trenches and dug in gun emplacements scattered among the bushes, but they are all abandoned, The Krauts have taken their weapons and fled.

The summit was well fortified for a strong defense, but how could the Krauts fight the white phosphorus demons? I can picture their agony in the night.

The rising sun is touching the wet plants with gold and the mountain air is clear. With the morning the terror of the night has vanished. We can see for miles across the valleys and ridges, but don't see the Germans. Yet, we know they aren't far away. They are close by and under cover.

The Krauts hide between the thick adobe walls of the farm houses where our bullets will not penetrate, and they turn the buildings into forts. The army has decided we can blast them out with an anti-tank weapon. Every squad will have a bazooka team.

No one wants to carry a bazooka. It is an awkward weapon, a hollow pipe over four feet long that trips you when you try to run. Marty must choose someone from our squad. Without hesitation and offering no explanation he chooses Ayers to be the unlucky one.

Ayers accepts the job philosophically without comment, but he asks me to be the other half of the team and carry the ammunition. Neither of us have had any experience with the weapon, although we each fired it once during our basic training.

To practice Ayers kneels on one knee with the bazooka resting on his shoulder. I load the rocket by pushing it into the rear of the tube and Ayers sights and pulls the trigger. We don't actually fire the rocket, but we have mastered the procedure.

Since it would be difficult to carry both a rifle and the bazooka, Ayers now carries a pistol on his belt in the same manner as the officers. It is strange to see him walking in front of me with his stove pipe. I must now carry a light pack with three of the rockets.

We are moving along a muddy road giving support to some tanks. They are creeping slowly forward, their turrets covered with branches for camouflage. Mixed with the tanks are some new model tank destroyers and I look at them with envy. They bring back memories of my first training with the tank destroyers. How angry I was when the army switched me to the infantry.

The tanks are nearing a hill and they leave the road to ascend it. The rain, which is once more falling from the steel gray sky, is making puddles in the road and softening up the hills. Our uniforms are soaking up the water, but we pay little attention. We are used to the smell of wet wool and the feel of it clinging to our skins.

The tanks are in trouble on the hill. The engines are racing and the tracks spinning, but the heavy machines just dig down into the mud. It is strange, for these are medium tanks and we have seen the massive German tiger tanks with their broad tracks churn their way up such grades sending the mud flying behind them.

Since the tanks are bogged down we receive orders to prepare to spend the night. Automatically we head for the nearest cover to find shelter from the rain and the only protection in the area is a small grove of Chestnut trees. The chestnuts are ripe and scattered all over the ground. We pick them up but don't know how to eat them.

Scotty and Malik have found something else. They have been exploring and return with two chickens, one brown and one white. The birds are screeching with fright, but both Malik and Scotty know how to handle them.

"We're going to have a chicken dinner," Scotty says, holding his chicken up by the feet.

"How are you going to kill them?" Wallace asks.

"Like this," Scotty answers, ringing the chicken's neck.

"Don't do that!" Wallace implores Malik who is about to kill the other chicken.

Malik ignores his plea and quickly rings the other chicken's head off.

"You shouldn't have done that!" Wallace wails. "Don't you know if you let a chicken die in your hands it'll make you nervous?" "We never do anything that makes us nervous," Martin interrupts -The roaring of the tank engines begins again. They are determined to get up the hill and we get another order to prepare to move out. Malik and Scotty reluctantly toss the dead chickens to the ground and pick up their gear.

We stand around in the rain with our equipment on, but nothing is moving. The tank treads are squealing and spinning, but they can't get any traction in the mud. We continue to stand waiting until it gets dark. A new order is passed down to us. We are to prepare to spend the night but be ready to move out quickly.

It is raining harder and I hate the thought of digging a hole in the mud, especially when we may be moving at any time. One of the chestnut trees is hollow and there is an opening just large enough for me to squeeze inside. Although the tree is leaning about forty-five degrees it is dry and hollow like a pipe. Compressed inside I try to get some sleep, but it is so cramped that I can't move my arms and I begin to get claustrophobia. The sounds of mortar shells landing nearby make me nervous. I am above ground level and if I should get hit in this tree who would find me?

The ground seems safer! Squirming out of the small hole I roll up in my shelter half to sleep in the mud.

All night the tanks continue to race their motors,, drawing enemy shellfire to the area. As the night progresses the mortars and artillery fire increase. It is becoming very active all around us. I am glad when the sleepless night ends and we move out in front of the tanks leaving them behind.

We meet four G.I.s leading an Italian civilian back toward the rear. The man has his hands tied behind his back and he looks terrified.

"I'd hate to be him," Denny says. "He hid some Krauts in the attic of a house and then told everyone that all the Germans were gone. When we set up a battalion headquarters there the Krauts sneaked down and took the major and his staff prisoner. Can you imagine what those guys are going to do to him?"

FOURTEEN

We all have a special sense, something from primitive days when man was lower on the evolutionary scale. It is the feeling of porcupine quills sticking in your spine, the urge to quickly turn your head when eyes are burrowing into your neck, the unexplained dread or uneasiness connected with certain places.

We are sitting among boulders as large as houses, sitting in the warm sun with our backs leaning against the rocks eating our rations. The front is quiet, and we are in reserve. We are following another platoon, ready to move up and give support if it is needed. It's better than being on the attack, so why are we all smothered with anxiety and nervousness? It is in everyone's face and in the depressed conversations. The air is heavy!

The strange feeling first comes over me as I rip open my K rations and toss the carton among the rocks. There are other cartons and tins scattered about. It is odd to see American trash. We are usually the first ones in an area, but the platoon we are following must have been here before. What a strange coincidence that they should have arrived among these boulders at mealtime and have chosen the identical spot to eat.

As I stare at this scattered trash a feeling comes over me that I have never felt before. I have no word to describe it, but it makes me shudder. Then I hear a rumor that there is a trap ahead. It is a dark, startling rumor that flies from nowhere, a dark bat lurching from one man to another. Who said it? Who could know what lies ahead? I look at one buddy after another to see who has suggested this thing. They all are sitting quietly eating the rations.

I turn to Marty, who is sitting next to me, but he is staring off into space with a blank look. As I study his gray-blue eyes I feel a chill go through me. He is staring at the beyond, and I see the look of eternity. Somehow I understand it and I turn my eyes away.

We do not take long to eat and are soon back climbing the trail again. Nearing the summit, we walk into a slight drizzle, and upon reaching the crest we are in the clouds. Patches of fog are hanging near the ground.

Again I feel that strange premonition of impending doom. Denny feels it too, for he motions for us to spread out into three squads and to advance in formation.

The fog is blurring the bushes and everywhere there is an absolute silence. Not a leaf is fluttering. Nothing is real.

What is that among the bushes? The dead body of a G.I.! There is another one sprawled beside a partially dug slit trench! We are walking through a grizzly scene with dead G.I.s all around us. Some are on their backs and others frozen in grotesque positions with their faces in the dirt.

One burns into my memory and shakes my nerves. He is on his back with both hands held up in front of his chest. His eyes are closed and he has a smile on his face.

Canteens and equipment are scattered all around. The men were taken by surprise as they dug their slit trenches.

I want to turn and run, but keep walking mechanically, hypnotically forward. We all stare at the savage scene in silence. This is the platoon we've been following. Are there any survivors? I see none. Once more the rumor of the trap runs through my mind.

The fog is growing dense, trying to hide the horror of the scene. We are cautiously forcing ourselves forward when the silence is shattered.

It is only a little sound, but it seems deafening.

Somewhere among the bushes and fog, close by, we hear a faint scraping sound. Someone is digging with a shovel.

Denny motions for Martin and me to investigate. Martin quickly sneaks forward, running lightly on the toes of his feet, and I follow close behind with my finger on the trigger of my rifle.

Abruptly, saying nothing, Martin whirls and races back past me. Spinning, without knowing what he has seen, I flee with him.

The day explodes! A machine gun opens up and I see the tracers flying by my side. Leaping to the right, I hear another machine gun and then another, mixed with the scattered blasts of hand grenades exploding.

In my haste to get back I stumble and roll. Crawling over the dead bodies and through the partially dug holes, I pull myself along the ground while the tracers fly all around.

"Over here!" Ayers yells, and I see his waving arms over by a small embankment.

Plunging toward him, with Ayers pulling on me, I tumble down the hill to safety. As I roll I see the bazooka shells fly out of my pack and bounce down the mountain.

"Forget them," Ayers says. "I fell over the bazooka and lost it up on top."

Six of us crouch down and watch the tracers racing around the top of the hill like savage bloodhounds. Ayers has found a bullet hole in my pack, and when I examine it I notice that there are streaks of blood on the canvas.

"It isn't my blood. I wasn't hit," I tell him. "It must have come from the bodies of the dead G.I.s."

"Those bazooka shells must have fallen out before that bullet hit your pack---lucky thing."

We call out to Denny, Marty and Martin, but there are no answers. Withdrawing farther down the mountain we can't find anyone from our company and when we call out there are no answers. How could everyone have vanished? Somewhere the company had to regroup.

It is easy to lose all sense of direction on the steep mountain in the fog. Continuing our search we come across a trail that leads down to a plateau. There is an isolated farmhouse on the level ground. As we near it a major comes out and yells to us.

"Where are you going?"

"We're trying to find our company," Ayers explains. "We walked into a trap and everyone scattered."

"Well get back up there," he shouts. "Your company is the only thing between here and the Germans. This is battalion headquarters."

"I think our company is scattered all over," Ayers says. "They're lost up there in the fog."

The major, himself, turns as white as the fog and grabs Ayer's arm.

"You have to make a stand! Wait! Wait! I'll get them on the radio."

He rushes into the building leaving the six of us outside leaning against the wall. After a few minutes he returns and says that our company is regrouping near the summit and they will send someone down to lead us to the area.

The man doesn't arrive until after dark when the fog is more dense than ever. Our morale drops even lower when we see he is someone we don't know.

"Probably a new replacement," Ayers whispers.

We have no choice but to trust our new guide as he leads us along a twisting trail through bushes and boulders. It doesn't seem possible our company is so far away! We walk on and on. Can the man be lost?

When we finally come to a squat, empty house that is huddled against the mountain our guide tells us to wait while he goes ahead to try to make contact with the company.

This seems a strange procedure to me. Why don't we go together? Night, cold and hunger are conducive to suspicious thinking. What if there are German patrols in the area? What if our company has been captured and this is all enemy territory? What if our guide is captured or gives us away? We stay alive by being cautious and suspicious. It is a fearsome wait.

Finally the guide returns.

"We're almost there. The company's just up ahead."

Everyone has assembled just below the crest of the hill near the Kraut machine guns. No one is digging in because it would make a noise. We join the rest of the company lying down on the sloping ground, but I'm too animal alert to sleep. My fear is that the Krauts will crawl over the hill and hurl their grenades down on top of us.

The dawn brings new fears. Out in the open we are exposed to sniper fire. To protect myself I move over among some bushes and quietly begin to dig a hole.

Denny tells us there is a survivor of the massacre, a lieutenant, and he is still lying up there. He is shot in the legs and can't walk. When our platoon advanced in the fog he called out a warning and that saved many from walking into the trap. Denny says he bent over and talked with him for a minute before we had to withdraw.

All morning more and more soldiers have been arriving. The entire battalion is going to make an assault and we don't know the enemy's strength.

The men arriving keep asking us if we have any rations. Some of them haven't eaten in three days, but we can't help them. We have no rations either. The Krauts are shelling the valley behind us so the supply trucks can't get through. All the roads and intersections are zeroed in!

Like eagles in an aerie we have a broad view of the beseiged valley. We watch the barrages below send up plumes of dust and we listen to the booming of the exploding shells.

Suddenly a piece of shrapnel bounces off my helmet. It does no damage since its force was spent by the great distance, but I am amazed that shrapnel can travel so far.

By late afternoon all of our men have arrived and the order is given to advance along a broad front. Ayers and Marty are beside me as we crawl over the crest of the hill and move into the area of the massacre. This time we stay close to the ground and make short runs, dropping to the ground frequently.

We draw close to the machine guns, but they are holding their fire and our nerves are taut. On and on we crawl with neither side firing. Soon we are crawling through the empty gun emplacements. The Krauts and their guns are gone!

When we find the wounded lieutenant he tells us the Krauts pulled back during the night. While the medics treat his legs and prepare to evacuate him to the hospital he tells the grim story of his platoon.

On a foggy afternoon the platoon reached the summit, their objective, unopposed. They checked the ground around the level area and found no Krauts so they began to prepare their defenses against a possible counter attack. Everyone was tired from the long advance. They had been working on the slit trenches for about a half hour when without warning their world came to an end.

From out of the fog and dripping bushes streams of tracers ripped into them from three directions as the machine guns raked the area. Grenades finished the attack.

The lieutenant alone had survived the quick attack, but he had been hit in both legs. One leg was broken. Over thirty men lay dead and the only sound he heard was that of German voices.

While the Krauts went among the bodies checking to make sure each man was dead, the lieutenant played dead. Then the Germans set to work digging, making gun emplacements, setting up their trap. One of the guns was only a few yards from where the lieutenant lay. He dared not move and in silence had to endure the pain of his throbbing leg.

Later the Krauts returned to search the bodies and take the water from the canteens. They rolled the lieutenant over and still he was able to remain convincingly dead.

All through the night the Krauts were vigilant, watching for any sign of the expected Americans. The lieutenant could only lie and suffer, daring not to try to crawl away. There was no hope that any movement would go unobserved.

Morning came once more and slowly passed. He wondered if death might not overtake him and all the suffering be in vain, but he couldn't give up hope.

Then, in the afternoon fog he saw shadowy figures from our platoon like phantoms in the mist. At first he wondered if he were having halucinations, but as the figures drew silently closer he saw they were G.I.s. Taking a chance, he motioned to Denny and when he leaned down warned him of the trap.

The Krauts stopped digging, the machine guns fired and the G.I.s fled into the fog. He had another night of waiting without food or water, but this time he had hope. Somewhere behind the foggy curtain the Americans were near and sometime soon they would come again. They knew he was there.

We do not stay on the crest of the mountain, but pursue these Krauts with a vengence! Moving down the slopes we can look back and see the crown still covered with clouds. That fog enabled the Krauts to sneak up and annihilate the platoon, but it also made it possible for us to escape the trap.

We are leaving a bad dream, but for our platoon it is a miracle. After walking right up to the Kraut machine guns we survived. There were no casualties.

I still do not understand the rumor of the trap. Was it telepathy, a message from the wounded lieutenant? Is a logical explanation possible?

FIFTEEN

All the mountain farmhouses are monotonous and alike--old buildings with tan adobe walls and tile roofs. I know we are advancing, but the similarity of the buildings creates the illusion that we are reliving each experience and are doomed to repeat each day over and over.

We are approaching one of these houses in our usual single file formation. For a change this one is not on a hill, but sits on sloping ground with a plowed field in front of it. We are advancing toward it from high ground so it is below us. However, we must cross that field to reach it.

The sight of the open area with no cover or ditches to protect us from sudden attack arouses fear and puts me on guard. Infantry men hate situations like this.

Walking on the furrowed earth is difficult. We are stumbling over the dry clods as if we are drunk as our line moves far out into the field.

We are blasted! Mortar shells are raining all over the field, crashing in our ears!

Instinctively we hug the ground and clutch at the furrows. My spine is quivering. The shells are hitting close and there's no protection. We search frantically with our eyes and simultaniously we all see some earthen mounds about one hundred yards from the house. Everyone is racing toward them!

There is not room for us all behind the mounds and since Wallace and I are toward the end of the line we are left out. The only other shelter is a shallow ditch that crosses the field in front of, and to the right of, the mounds. In desperation Wallace and I plunge into this small depression, but the ditch is so shallow we can barely get below ground level.

To terrify us more, the Krauts open fire from the house using rifles and machine guns. I am squeezing myself down as far as possible, afraid to move. Wallace has some bushes in front of him and this gives him confidence. I look over and see him climbing out on a large boulder.

"What are you doing?" I yell at him. "Get down!"

"There are bushes here," he says. "I can see the Krauts."

"If you can see them, they can see you!"

"Fire on the house!" Denny yells. "Everyone bring maximum fire on the house!"

Being in direct sight of the enemy, I don't dare raise up. I fire my rifle without sighting, holding it up and aiming at the windows.

The Kraut machine guns are peppering the field and our rifles and B.A.R.s are chipping away at the house.

"Smack!" Wallace falls off of the rock.

Grabbing him, I drag him toward me. I can see blood running down the side of his head.

Still conscious, he says, "I'm hit!"

I can see a wound in his cheek and he's bleeding behind the ear also. Unsnapping his first aid packet from his belt I try to get the sulfa powder out. I don't know how to stop the bleeding from such a wound, and my fingers are in the way as I try to apply the bandage.

"Medic!" I yell. "Medic! A man's hit!"

"Hurry up!" Wallace says as I fumble some more, having difficulty because we are both flat on our stomachs afraid to rise up. I'm not getting anywhere and am fighting back a sense of panic. I have to stop the rapid bleeding.

Desperate and frustrated, I'm still struggling when a figure comes racing through a hale of bullets and drops beside me. Thank God it's Allen! Even though he wears the red cross how did he get through without being hit? It seems impossible! And how did he have the courage to try?

With cool efficiency Allen takes over the first aid while I watch with amazement.

"They're taking off," Marty shouts.

It is true. The Krauts, badly ounumbered, are abandoning the house and running off down the slope.

"Let's go!" Denny yells, and we surge forward after the fleeing Krauts in one ragged wave. By the time we reach the house the enemy has melted into the shrubbery on the next hill.

I watch Wallace being carried to the rear on a litter and I think of the day he led me and the other replacements up to the front for the first time. He had told us that every time he went up to the line he was more scared. He had a lot of combat experience, but he made a mistake. In combat the first mistake could be fatal, and none of us are perfect. Who knows what we we may do? It's a depressing thought!

We are all sick of the rain and glad that at last we can feel the warm sun and see the mountains through clear air. The squad is walking single file through a valley on a dusty road. A shot rings out! Truett pitches forward!

Dropping along the road we all study the brush covered mountain. Somewhere up there a sniper is hiding with a telescopic sight. There's no chance of spotting him.

Why did he choose Truett? He was walking along toward the middle of the squad.

The medics rush Truett back to an aid station and the rest of us stay away from the road and continue by walking through the brush. When we stop to dig in for the night Scotty goes back to the aid station to see how his buddy is doing.

Although Truett is badly hurt, he demands to know where Scotty has been and asks why he didn't come sooner. He accuses Scotty of deserting his buddy when he needed him.

The medic says Truett has been crying and calling for Scotty all afternoon.

Scotty, who is usually quiet and says very little, tries to explain that he couldn't leave the squad during a combat operation, but Truett won't listen. Again he accuses Scotty of deserting him. Then Truett abrubtly dies!

We all feel bad about losing a buddy who has been with us so long, and when we hear the story from the medic we mourn for Scotty too. All night he is completely silent.

Sixteen

Confidence! What can be more important to our morale? We have to rely on each other as we go about this deadly business every day. We soon learn who we can depend on when our lives are at stake.

We have confidence in our leaders, like platoon sergeant Denny who is cool and dedicated to the job in battle. He never panics or gets angry and is never recklessly excited. He is always thinking, with his mind on the present objective. He is concerned about his men, yet expecting everyone to do his part. Denny calmly takes great risks himself with a fatalistic, dedicated attitude. The war will be won by men like Denny. Although we hate everything about the war, we do what we have to do under his leadership.

We have confidence in our officers too, especially our company commander. Captain Mathews. We know he is a graduate of West Point, well trained for the job he is doing. Like Denny he is always cool and unruffled no matter how devastating the battle. We have seen his cautious approach in battle and know he is not a glory seeker. He takes great personal risks and always shows concern for his men.

We have confidence in Lieutenant James who was a sergeant before he received a commission in the field. He is still one of us and deals with us in a democratic manner. We also had confidence in Lieutenant Lyons before he was so abruptly killed.

Now everything is changed, our confidence shaken. Battalion headquarters has decided our platoon is to be temporarily separated frcin our company and attached to A Company. This will give A Company added strength as they move into a very active area.

We are uneasy and apprehensive about this change since we don't know the A Company officers or men. Of course we accept the sudden change without comment. Every man does his own thinking.

All I know of A Company is that their CO. is a long legged first lieutenant who sometimes led the whole battalion on a fast hike when we were in training at Villa Magna. I doubt if he'll lead us that fast in combat.

As A Company starts down the road our platoon falls in at the end of the line. We allow a few yards to separate us so we look like a different unit. We feel no hostility, it is just that each company is a separate unit socially as well as in organization. Whenever the battalion sets up a bivouac each company has its own area. The companies are close by, but there is little contact between the men. It just happens that way.

Led by Denny, we follow A Company along a dusty country road that cuts through a fertile mountain valley. There are fences and tall weeds along the road, and beyond these are corn and wheat fields. Everything has been harvested for the year and the fields are bare.

We continue for several hours and in the mid afternoon we are passing a farmhouse that is built so close to the road that we can touch its dirty plastered walls as we go by. Here the line stops and we don't know why. Denny walks ahead to talk with the A Company officers. Soon he returns and explains what is happening.

"They want us to dig in for the night in the field across the road from this house. All of A Company will dig trenches in that next field up the road."

We are in a scenic place with many tall trees bordering the field. The afternoon sun is splashing gold on the surrounding hills and mountains.

The soil here is dark and rich and since it is still moist from the recent rains, we find the digging is easy. Ayers and I soon have a very large slit trench, over six feet long and three feet deep. It is wide enough for us both to lie down side by side.

After all the exertion we are warm and we're cooling off in the long shadows of the trees when Denny calls for the radio man.

"I'm going over to the house to set up a command post," he explains. "I'll radio the company and see if there are any further instructions. If you need me for anything send a runner."

We watch Denny and the radio man go into the house, and in a few minutes Denny comes out again and calls for some of us to come over on the double.

When we reach him we can see he is excited and anxious.

"When we opened that door we walked into a room full of Krauts. We were facing five machine guns with twenty-five Krauts behind them. They were relaxed and smoking. As soon as they saw us they raised their hands. One of the Krauts who spoke English said they had been waiting to surrender."

"What a snafu mess," Ayers says. "Those Krauts could have cut us down while we were digging in. They had a direct line of fire."

Thinking about how easily we could have all been massacred demoralizes me. I am thankful we were spared, but I'm angry. We were at the end of the line and all of A Company filed by the house before we reached it. It is hard to believe they didn't have advance scouts check the house. It is standard procedure!

Some of our men are laughing about the ridiculous situation, but I'm feeling depressed and wondering how long we can go on being lucky.

"It wasn't our time!" Marty says. "If the bullet has your name on it, that's all she wrote!"

"That's A Company," Ayers says, shaking his head.

"Be sure to stay in your holes at chow time," Denny warns. "Those Krauts had a radio! Their artillery knows G.I.s hate to eat in their holes and tonight they might try to mix some shrapnel with your rations."

Five o'clock comes. Six and seven pass and it remains quiet. The sun is setting--that means it is morning at home. The darkness is beginning to close in around us and everything is still. There isn't even a trigger happy Kraut with a machine gun firing in the distance.

All at once the hill to our left coughs dirt into the air as it is hit by a barrage. This is followed by a series of more distant booms. Then it is silent once more.

Those were damn big shells," Ayers says. "Like from a railroad gun."

The closeness of the shell fire on the neighboring hill has made us nervous, so we keep low in our trenches. Things don't feel right.

Hell is opening up all around us! The noise is deafening! It's a massive earthquake and the earth is erupting in geysers of dirt!

Shell after shell is thundering into the field! Ayers and I are flat on our stomachs, faces down, with our hands clasped over the back of our necks. The giant blasts send the shrapnel zinging, whistling and screaming. We are in the middle of it. We feel what is happening, but see nothing with our eyes tightly shut, calling upon God to protect us.

We are quivering, paralyzed with fright, unable to think, knowing that each second may be our last. The air is so acrid and choking with burnt powder that we can hardly breathe, and still the earth continues to belch and buck!

Once more the shell fire switches back to the neighboring hill, pulverizing it again. After that the shelling stops.

"Keep alert!" Ayers says. "After a shelling they'll attack. They do this!"

I take my rifle in my hand, but Ayers puts his hand on the back of my neck and pushes me down.

"Keep down! They may shell us some more!"

My mind is a flash of light! I hear an ocean roar! I'm flying through the air and the ground is rearing up to meet me. I am on my knees on the plowed ground. Staggering to my feet, I see acrid smoke hanging around me like a cloud. I stand dazed until someone grabs my ankle.

"In here!" a voice yells, and I see a hand reaching out of a slit trench pulling me toward it.

I stumble into the trench and squeeze in with three other men. We lay jammed together as the shelling continues. I put my head down and touch the ground with the front of my helmet. My body relaxes and I feel myself going to sleep.

My eyes open. The sun is streaming in on my face and I am alone in the slit trench, lying on my back looking at the blue sky. Sitting up, I see my buddies walking around the devastated field gathering up their equipment.

"Hey," one yells at me. "Denny just gave the order to prepare to move out."

I can't believe the transformation around me. Only the shattered trunks of the tall trees remain. The field is a desert of craters within craters. Debris and equipment is scattered all over.

Looking down I see that I still clutch the stock of my rifle in my hand, but the stock is all I have. Only a piece of wood and the trigger assembly remain. All the rest has been blown away!

There is no sign of the hole that Ayers and I dug, and none of our ammunition or equipment remain.

"What happened to Ayers?" I ask.

"The medics took him to the hospital. He was shell shocked."

Denny was right about those Krauts in the house, I am thinking. They radioed our position. We were hit dead center!

I throw down the shattered remains of my rifle and suddenly feel naked. I have two free hands and that isn't right. I can't be defenseless at the front. I have to have a weapon!

With such heavy casualties, there must be something laying around.

Anxiously I walk around the field picking at pieces of equipment, but I can't find a rifle. There are no weapons anywhere.

The men are forming a line, ready to leave. As I hasten to join them my eye catches a glimpse of something metal in the brush by the side of the road. It's a tommy gun! It has a full clip of ammo in it, but I don't see any more around. That could be a problem. The rifles are all thirty caliber, but the tommy gun takes forty-five caliber ammunition.

I sling the tommy gun over my shoulder. At least it's a weapon, although I would prefer a rifle.

Denny leads us to the next field to join A Company, but when we arrive we find all the holes are deserted. There's no sign of anyone. Why would they leave without telling us? It is very strange.

"Everybody in A Company couldn't have forgotten us," Marty says.

"Not likely," Denny agrees.

We can see a church about two hundred yards down the road and Denny thinks A Company may have moved over to it during the night. Cautiously we start forward to check it out.

Certainly A Company has been in the church, for inside the sanctuary, in a corner, all of their equipment is stacked. There are bed rolls, packs and ammunition, but no weapons.

"What does it mean?" I ask.

"Damn! They must have been captured," Martin says.

"The whole company?" I ask in disbelief. "They were dug in all over the field and it was dark. How could the Krauts get everybody?"

I am thinking of what Ayers said about the Krauts infiltrating after a barrage. Yet, we heard no shots fired.

"In the dark they crawl up to your hole and point a rifle at you. Then they motion for you to follow," Marty says.

"I guess they didn't know about us," Martin says.

"It could have happened when we were pinned down by the barrage," Malik suggests. "That's why we didn't hear anything."

"They may have shelled our field to scare them and keep them in their holes," Marty agrees. "They may not have shelled A Company. The Krauts wouldn't shell the field where their own men were infiltrating."

All this is hard for me to imagine. We really don't know how A Company was captured. While we are talking about it, one of our platoon scouts comes running in excited.

"I was walking a few yards up the road," he says, "when all of a sudden a Jerry stood up and surrendered. He was just a few feet from me and he had a machine gun. I didn't even see him!"

"Well," Denny says, "you were just lucky."

"There are a lot more Jerries up the road," the scout adds.

Denny listens and then calls our company on the radio. He gives a report to Captain Mathews and also tells him of our suspicions about A Company. Captain Mathews tells him to bring the platoon back to rejoin our company.

As I leave the church I look again at all the equipment and I'm wondering where the long legged lieutenant and all his men are now.

The small house reminds me of a gray toad crouching right beside the road. It is built of stone with a low slanting roof. Inside there is just one room and the only furniture is a white table with a German lueger lying on it.

We gather around and carefully study the gun.

"It looks new," Marty says. "I'd love to have that one."

He doesn't pick it up. None of us touch it. We know the Germans study our habits and set clever booby-traps. The lueger looks alright and we do not see any hidden charges, but the pistol remains on the table, a prize not worth the risk. We don't understand why the Krauts have abandoned the house and left the lueger so neatly behind.

Our platoon was the first to reach the house, but we are soon joined by the rest of the company. All squeezed into the tiny room, we are crowded together on the floor like the pieces of a jigsaw puzzle.

The afternoon is hot and the air in the room is stuffy from the breathing of so many people. We are all tired and there is no talking. The only sound is the regular, heavy breathing, and it is like a lullaby to me.

I am awakened by the grating of the door. Lieutenant James has come in and he is furious.

"You were all asleep!" he screams in a hoarse whisper. "Do you want to be captured or killed? The Krauts are just up the road."

The Krauts are so near that he is afraid to speak in a normal voice, so pointing to four of us he motions for us to follow him. He is going to try to contact the artillery by radio and while he is doing this he wants us to go back down the road to meet a jeep that is bringing up rations. We walk for over two miles and it is almost dark before we find the supply jeep. Each of us is given a carton of K rations to take back to the house.

On our way back we come across a litter lying in the road with a dead G.I. on it. Around it are the dead bodies of the four medics who were carrying it. An artillery shell has wiped them all out.

When we reach the house we tear open the cartons and toss each man a ration. Everyone is hungry and it doesn't take long for the biscuits and tins of stew to disappear.

Outside, the full moon has turned the brown fields into a gray sea. Across that sea the two houses occupied by the Krauts are dark and quiet. The open windows look like black caves in the gray walls.

All afternoon we saw no sign of the Krauts, but G-2 reported they are in the houses. They also reported that they had seen some white flags earlier and thought some Germans might want to surrender. However, we have seen no sign of any flags.

Now that it is dark we are planning to advance across the field and attack, but the bright moonlight will make this difficult. If the houses are not deserted the Krauts have an excellent field of fire across the flat land. Certainly they can see anyone who tries to cross the field.

The entire company forms a line along the edge of the field and Denny tells us we are to crawl across slowly. By staying close to the ground we may be undetected. First, however, a patrol is being sent out to see if it will draw any fire.

While the rest of us lie with our guns aimed at the two houses, the men of the patrol walk cautiously out into the field. They are half crouched, walking lightly and quickly toward the threatening barrier.

"Boom!" The ground shakes and a column of black smoke shoots up from the field, forming a puff of smoke in the moonlight. What is it? We can't see the patrol.

The black smoke is still drifting across the sky when Denny tells us what we have just seen. The sergeant leading the patrol stepped on a mine and was blown to pieces. The second man was also killed and the other three men were wounded.

We are already nervous about crawling across the field, but now, knowing it is a mine field, we are terrified. We hope the plan will now be changed, but it isn't.

"Be prepared to start," Denny says.

Everyone is flat on the ground along the edge of the field. Beside me are Marty, Martin, Rule, Malik, Scotty and Davis. Our eyes are on that gray sea of furrows that seems frozen in the moonlight. The two buildings beyond, showing no signs of life, look like impassive boulders.

With dread we await the order to advance. Although our instincts for self preservation are crying out in protest, we know we must show courage and hope we have the self discipline to be brave. Mentally we must each face destiny in his own way. I say a silent prayer.

"Where's your ammo?" Denny is looking at me, noting that I have no bandoliers over my shoulders.

I tell him about losing the ammunition and my rifle during the barrage.

"I searched around until I found a tommy gun with one clip. That's all I have."

"We've set up a machine gun at the corner of the field to cover the advance," Denny says. "Go over there and set up a position to protect the flank. A tommy gun would be good for that."

It is a reprieve! Quickly I jump up and run over to the machine gun to place myself between it and the road. As I pass Denny our eyes meet. We both know he has given me a break.

The order is given to advance and the line of men slowly disappears into the field. In spite of the moonlight I can't follow the movements. Since there is no firing from the house, the machine gun remains silent. I wonder if the Krauts are aware of what is happening.

How long will it take the men to cross the field? We wait nervously. Minutes go by—still no sign of the action.

"Someone's coming down the road," one of the gunners says.

Straining my eyes I pick up a man running toward us. Is he a G.I.? We can't tell. He is getting close and we are still undecided.

"All's clear!" he shouts. "No Jerries. They've left."

Avoiding the field, we pick up the gun and the ammo and follow the runner back down the road to the houses. Inside, everyone is nervously inspecting the rooms.

Remembering the mines in the field, we fear booby traps and trip wires inside. Since we dare not light a candle or use a light, it seems safer to leave the houses and move along the road.

Our scouts report there is another empty house just ahead. Artillery shells are falling just beyond it, so we move into the building and send out a scouting patrol to investigate the area.

Two of us are on lookout at the window in the attic, and I am nervous. With me is a new replacement whose name I don't remember, and he is like a puppy dog, following me around trusting me to do the right thing.

The house has just recently been abandoned by the enemy and our platoon, after searching all the rooms in the large two story building, is using it as a place to rest. The men are sleeping on the first floor.

Up in the attic there is just one big window, and as usual in Italian farmhouses, there is no glass. Outside the landscape is very bright, so we sit back from the window to prevent our equipment from reflecting the moonlight. In the dark shadows we can hardly see each other.

I hate to have my back to the darkness inside, for I can imagine some Kraut still hiding in some tiny nook. We couldn't use a light to inspect the rooms carefully. I can't rationally explain why it makes me uneasy and nervous to be in a house at the front. I prefer a camouflaged slit trench out in a field.

Any outpost at night is a lonely and tense place. The rest of the men are sleeping and depending on the lookouts to be responsible. We especially worry when it is too dark to see anything. Then the lonely lookout listens to the strange noises of the night and fights off the imaginary visions created by his own eyes.

This night in the attic is as cold and isolated as usual, but the bright moonlight makes it easy to observe the quiet land that resembles a ruffled blanket. Right beside the house there is a deep canyon with a dry stream bed. The rocks in the channel are gray and white in the moonlight.

The front is quiet and the only sound is the drone of a plane's engines. The noise is growing louder and I recognize the peculiar sound of the motor, as if it is missing. It is a German plane.

"It's probably Bed Check Charley," I tell the new replacement. "He flies over evey night about ten. He does a little strafing, drops a few bombs and then flies on. If you hear him just lie still until he leaves. If you fire on him you'll give your position away—and that's what he wants. He'll radio the artillery and you'll catch hell."

The plane is overhead. One plane alone. I sit still and alert, listening. I hear a click and my heart stops beating. He's released a bomb.

A tremendous blast shatters the creek bed down in the canyon.

"That bomb was meant for us," I tell my buddy. "He barely missed. Thank God for the canyon. If there had been level land out there we'd have caught the full force of the blast."

The plane is circling. I sit tensely waiting, expecting some strafing to follow. The fifty caliber bullets will easily go through the roof of the house.

Again and again the plane circles, but the circles are growing larger. The motor is fading away.

Wide awake now, we both nervously watch from the window. Things may not be as peaceful out there as they look. It is near midnight when a runner comes up to tell us the company has received orders to move to another sector to give added strength in a lively area.

We walk through the night for several miles before stopping to dig slit trenches on a brush covered slope. While we are digging several German planes are cruising overhead.

Black puffs of smoke burst in the sky. Is it flak from our distant anti-aircraft batteries or is it Kraut artillery firing air burst shells? When the Krauts fire these there is no protection. The shrapnel rains down into the slit trenches.

It is three in the morning before we have finally finished digging the trenches.

"New orders," Denny says. "We're to go back to the house and stay in hiding all day."

We accept the change without comment, although we suspect it is because of the German planes.

To return to the farm we follow a road that is lined with tall trees. Since these are on both sides of the road, our column is divided with half walking on each side. We stay close to the tree trunks and under the spreading branches. It is warm like a summer night and it is easy walking on the road.

I am getting very tired and am thinking how nice it will be to get back to the house and sleep, when I am shocked from my dream by the sound of a diving plane. My first thought is that he's going to strafe us. Instinctively I look for cover.

Just beyond the trees are rows of slit trenches dug by the Krauts before they pulled back. They look secure, but I'm afraid of anything left by the Krauts.

"Into the fields," Captain Mathews shouts. Racing away from the road, we scatter into the fields, losing ourselves among the three feet high weeds. We all drop to the ground, keeping our faces down to minimize any reflections from the bright moon.

The plane levels off and sweeps along the road just above the tree tops. He peppers the road with anti-personnel bombs that go off like strings of fire crackers.

There is no strafing. The plane pulls up and drones away. We slowly reassemble on the road to continue our march. Back in the shadows I am amazed the plane could have spotted us from the air.

"Captain Mathews gave a good order," Marty says. "The Krauts sometimes put mines in the bottom of their slit trenches."

"On a road like this they like to put a charge on a tree and run a trip wire across to the other side," Martin warns. "I hope the guys at the head of the line are watching where they're walking."

It is just before dawn when we reach the house. If the Kraut artillery doesn't know we're here, we'll get some rest.

SEVENTEEN

Psychologists tell us the sex drive is second only to the hunger drive, but at the front we are too tired and tense to give much thought to either.

We expect nothing but the same K rations every day and are so sick of them that eating has become a thoughtless necessity. There are three kinds of rations, chopped ham and eggs, a tin of cheese and a tin of stew. Day after day we have the same three. I often eat only one of them a day, trying a different one each time. The cheese I like the least for it still reminds me of the smell of the dead German that first day at the front. Although I eat very little, I am rarely hungry.

On rare occasions we find eggs at a farmhouse. Then, if possible, we boil them and it is a real treat. Sometimes we find even better things.

It is a night of heavy rain and we have "walked for miles to join the rest of the battalion in a large farmhouse. Our company is the last to arrive and when we enter the building we find men sleeping all over the floors in a crazy mosaic. Every room is carpeted with sleeping bodies. The building is packed to capacity.

Ayers has just returned from the hospital after being shell shocked, so he goes with me from room to room looking for a place to relax. Whenever we try to squeeze in someplace there are loud complaints from the men already there. In the entire building we can't find room enough for either of us to sit down.

"There's a barn out in back," I suggest. "It looked like a big one when we walked past."

"O.K.," Ayers agrees. "Let's try it."

It is not an original idea we find, for the barn is full of people. Many men from our company are snuggled down in the hay in the loft. Climbing up, we find there is still room for us.

Lying on our backs we can look up at the rickety roof made of thin tiles. The stars in the night sky are visible through many cracks.

"This place looks like it could fall down without any help," Ayers says.

I agree with him, but close my eyes to shut out the disturbing scene and to try to relax.

Some shells land near by and the building quivers.

"I don't like this a bit," Ayers says.

I don't answer him, but I feel uneasy.

Another shell lands close enough to throw some shrapnel onto the roof and the broken pieces of tile trickle down.

"I'm not staying here!" Ayers sits up. "That tile can cut you up."

I start to object because it is so warm and comfortable in the hay, but I know he's right. In the darkness we crawl over the bodies of many complaining buddies as we struggle to reach the ladder down.

Back in the house we are confronted with the same problem as before.

With no place to stretch out, we sit sandwiched between some sleeping men and the wall. When two of them have to get up to go on outpost we quickly move into their spots.

The air reeks with the smell of wet wool and warm bodies. It is a fitful sleep for me, for I am constantly awakened by shells landing near the house. Each time, I listen to the heavy breathing for awhile before dozing off again. My body is cramped and stiff from being forced into the same position for so long.

A shot rings out and I am instantly awake! It came from just outside the door, and is quickly followed by a second one.

Creeping to the door, I peek out over the stiff body of a long dead Jerry. The rain has stopped and a foggy mist hangs around the house. In the early morning light I see a solitary figure crouching low and creeping slowly toward a flock of turkeys. The man is holding a pistol out in front of him and as he nears a large turkey he fires again. The bird drops dead and the noise sends the rest of the flock fleeing in wild disorder in all directions. Of course most of them are doomed. Soon other G.I.s will join the hunt.

Ayers has found a large iron pot, and I make the second great discovery. The attic is filled with potatoes.

The problem, as usual, is how to cook the bird. The Krauts are only a half mile up the hill and any escaping smoke will bring a rain of artillery shells down on the house. Yet, we are determined to make the most of what fate has brought us.

Everyone joins in to prepare the feast. Blankets are hung over all the windows and doors, and more blankets are stuffed up the chimney.

There are no objections when Ayers brings in some wood and builds a fire in the middle of the brick floor. The pot is soon boiling.

Other G.I.s are bringing in dead turkeys and building fires. The room is filled with smoke that curls up, sweeps back and is compressed into layers. As it grows thicker and denser we sit coughing with tears streaming down our faces. Yet, no one wants the torture stopped.

Ayers has taken over as cook, checking the potatoes and sticking a knife into the meat. Finally, with a broad smile, he announces that dinner is ready. He personally serves everyone in the squad a generous portion of meat, potatoes and hot broth.

The hot meal under our belts lifts our morale. For the moment it is all that matters. We live in the present. Even somber Malik is smiling again.

The marks and scratches on our knuckles and hands are the visible records of the endless slit trenches we have dug in the rocky soil. Daily and hourly we are moving from ridge to ridge, valley to valley, farm to farm—and each time we stop we dig more slit trenches. Sometimes we dig two or three in a twenty-four hour period. No matter how tired we are, we dig in before resting. No one ever suggests we skip this ritual.

We dig slit trenches not because we are told to do it, for our officers never mention it. We dig because we are afraid of what will happen to us if we don't. We have seen the bodies blown apart and the wounded with missing arms and legs.

There are many terrible ways to be maimed and still survive. An officer told us that the injury most feared by G.I.s is to have his testicles crushed or his sex organs destroyed. Who can give priorities to the massive wounds possible or rate paralysis above blindness?

"I'd rather not go back at all than go back like that!" These are words we all say. Do we really mean it? How can we know for sure? Yet, I feel death is not the worst that can happen.

Ayers and I have been a good team—buddies, but since we were blown out of a hole things are changing. When he returned from the hospital, of course we teamed up again. I can understand why he is more nervous and jumpy. Shell shock will do that to a man. He is also more superstitious, but that isn't a special fault. Most combat soldiers are superstitious.

When you survive a battle you are afraid to change anything for fear it may change your luck. If you wore two grenades on your shoulder straps, then you must have two again. If you have a medalion or a four leaf clover, then you must be sure you still have it.

I fight against this, telling myself there has to be more to my survival than what I say or do, or what good luck charms I may carry. Ayers isn't that way.

We have been digging a slit trench for over an hour and finally have a deep hole. Before we can climb into it Ayers puts down his shovel and shakes his head.

"It isn't safe! We'll have to dig another hole over by that rock."

This demoralizes me, but I know I will not be able to relax knowing that Ayers has a hunch the hole isn't safe. Starting all over again, we dig another trench in the spot he has picked out.

By the time we are finished I am dead tired and climb down inside ready to stretch out. Ayers is standing by the hole studying it.

"This place is as safe as anywhere around," I tell him.

"Why did you say that?" he shouts. "Never say that! Now we can't stay here. We'll have to dig another hole."

"Not me! We've dug two already, and that's the limit for me. If we keep this up we'll never get any rest."

"I'm not staying here," Ayers says, picking up his gear and walking away.

I watch him go, but I can't bring myself to follow this time. A short distance away he digs another hole alone.

It is a quiet night with no artillery in the area. In the morning Ayers teams up with Shorty, a new replacement. I look around for someone who needs a buddy and I find Rule is digging in alone.

Rule has been with the squad for a long time, but has not formed any definite attachments. Recently he was digging in with a replacement, but his partner was wounded and went to the hospital

Our platoon moves forward again and when we stop to dig trenches we are on the southern slope of another hill. It is raining and we are digging in the mud as the little puddles form all around us.

Rule is from Minnesota and built like someone who could cut timber and split logs. He is big boned, tall and strong. With him shoveling out the dirt we have a deep hole in a hurry. The trench is so large that we can stretch a shelter half over the top to keep the rain out and still sit up with a foot of clearance above our heads.

I am glad we are deep because mortars have been hitting in the area. When Rule and I were looking for a place to dig we saw the bodies of several G.I.s on the hill.

I noticed one that looked too young to be in the army. I looked at the handsome face and slim body lying in the mud and I saw the gold wedding band on the frozen, stiff finger of the left hand. Being so young, he probably married his high school sweetheart. She doesn't know it yet, but she's a very young widow.

Rule and I are sitting in our hole listening to the mortar shells exploding, and I am thinking how he could pass for a German soldier with his blond hair and blue eyes. He is so fair he usually has a red complexion.

"A man's hit!" someone yells. "We need help to carry a wounded man!"

"Let's go help them," Rule says.

He is already out of the trench and starting up the slope. Automatically I follow him. We walk and slip along in the mud for about ten yards.

A giant hand slaps me to the ground! Boom! I hear the shattering blast while I am flat on my back.

A G.I. comes running over and puts his hand on my shoulder.

"How bad are you hurt?" he asks.

"I don't know," I give a dazed answer. "Something cut me here."

I point to my collar bone where there is a stinging sensation. When I touch it there's blood on my hand.

He studies the injury carefully.

"I think it's just skinned, but you better have the medics check it."

"Where's Rule?" I ask.

Rule is lying several yards away and the platoon medic is bent over him. Two other G.I.s are standing by to help.

"He's dead," Allen says, standing up. "Killed instantly by the blast."

Then Allen turns to me and checks my collar bone.

"It looks like a piece of shrapnel sliced across you. It just took the skin off, but you'd better go back to the aid station and have it bandaged."

"I was right beside Rule," I tell him.

"It was a mortar," Allen nods. "He was between you and the blast."

"So quick! We just left our hole."

I start for the aid station but I'm thinking of Rule. I hardly knew him, yet, I felt very much at ease around him, like we'd been friends for a long time. By the way he talked and his concern for others I'm sure he came from a good family. He always seemed quiet, but not shy—a gentle person. He died trying to help someone he didn't know. At least he's out of this savage existence and misery, and he didn't suffer.

Before going on to the aid station I find Marty and tell him what happened to Rule. Marty accepts the news without comment. His squad is always getting replacements.

"I think maybe I should go to the aid station with you," he says. "I've got a discharge from my penis. I'll show you."

He unzips his pants and I look at the traces of pus as he milks it down.

"What do you think?" he asks.

"You'd better go," I agree.

Together we walk to the aid station which is in a house about one hundred yards down the mountain to the rear. There the medic dresses my wound, and while he is putting the bandage on, I tell him I'm feeling very weak. With that he shoves a thermometer into my mouth.

"You have a temperature of 101," he says. "If it were 102 I'd send you to the hospital. If you feel worse come back and I'll check it again."

"I didn't expect to go to the hospital," I tell him, "but I can't remember very many times in my life when I had a temperature of 102, even when I was real sick."

"That's army regulations. I can't take anyone off the front unless his temperature is 102 or higher."

With Marty it is different. Any discharge from the penis is considered clap (gonorrhea), and that means the hospital.

"How could it be V.D.?" Marty whispers to me. "I haven't had any sex since I've been in Italy."

Back in my hole, I feel sicker than ever, and my legs ache. I think of Rule again. Jesus said there is no greater love than for a man to give his life for a friend. Rule lost his life trying to help a stranger.

The following morning, in a drizzle, we move on up the mountain. For the first time I have difficulty keeping up.

Eighteen

Up and then down--then up again! Day after day we are fighting across a roller coaster. Always advancing toward that endless parade of ridges, we find each one like the others, an armed barrier. We lose our sense of place and all sense of time.

Like vultures in well prepared -nests the Krauts wait, using their high powered binoculars to watch us. Single file, in long lines we crawl over the rough terrain like ants.

The intersections of the roads and trails are traps, marked well in advance for the artillery. Sniper's eyes with telescopic sights peer from hidden dens on the brush covered slopes. Long before we reach the entrenched Krauts we are harassed by screaming mortars and ripping machine guns that we call paper cutters.

It has become too costly to advance by daylight, so we change our tactics and advance more at night. We move through a shadowy world of black trees and gray boulders, approaching darkened farm buildings with the stealth of burglars.

We have been advancing all night, and spent the last few hours before dawn slipping and sliding down a steep mountain. I am feeling better again. It is amazing how resilient the human body can be. What punishment it can sustain!

Hoping to remain undetected in the daylight, we seek refuge in a three story farm house that is on the edge of the valley and looks like a tall box.

Captain Mathews sends me, with a nameless replacement, to the third floor to set up a lookout. From there we have an excellent view to the north.

We are no sooner settled in this crows nest then the house shakes violently as an artillery shell explodes in the yard. The first blast is followed by a second one that sends shrapnel through the windows to gouge the walls. The plaster is chipped from the ceiling and falls around us.

"Those shells are aimed at this house!" I exclaim. "The Krauts know we're here!"

"This third floor is a hell of a place to be," my new buddy says.

When another shell takes a piece of the roof off, we decide it is time to head for the lower floors. When we report to Captain Mathews he agrees the third floor is too dangerous. He tells us to forget the outpost, so we join the rest of the company which is crowded together on the first floor.

Like many Italian farms this is the stable. The two floors above are the living quarters.

In one corner of the stable, on a pile of straw, the owners of the house, an Italian family, are huddled together. The woman is fingering her rosary and praying softly. The two children are lying quietly beside their father in the hay.

Captain Mathews is talking to the major at battalion headquarters on the radio. We can hear the major demanding an immediate attack on the enemy, while Captain Mathews is insisting it would be suicide to go outside during the barrage.

The house rumbles and quivers as shells hit the third floor. Great pieces of plaster and sand are filtering down all around us. Both the major and the captain are getting angry as the major is shouting that we must advance immediately.

"Can't you hear the shelling on the radio?" Captain Mathews asks. "I can hardly hear you because the shells are hitting the house."

The major admits it sounds bad, but still demands an immediate advance. Captain Mathews is equally stubborn, opposing any move until the barrage subsides. He insists that any other action would cause heavy casualties and accomplish nothing.

All around the radio are the serious faces of the men in the company who are listening silently, sweating out the barrage. My respect for the captain is going even higher. Why won't a major in the rear accept the advice of a West Point trained officer who is on the spot?

Finally the intensity of the barrage is tapering off, and even though some shells are still falling Captain Mathews starts the evacuation of the house. It is too risky for us all to leave at once, so one man at a time is sent running out and down the road. There are long, irregular intervals between the men. Only one man can be killed by one shell!

Passively I await my turn, and when I am sent running I can't see the man who has gone ahead. I try to run low, staying close to the tall weeds and fences that border the road.

Everything is going fine until I come to a fork in the road. I am completely confused and there is no one stationed there to direct us.

It is too risky to wait out in the open, so I have to make a quick decision. Feeling very much alone, I follow the left fork because the weeds offer more concealment. I see no G.I.s anywhere and fear I could blunder into the Kraut positions.

My anxiety is relieved when I stumble upon a wounded G.I. who is lying be the side of the road. Raising an arm, he points to the direction the others have gone.

Cutting across a field, I see some trenches at the far end and spot the top of an American helmet in one of them. Racing and zig-zagging across the corn stubble, I dive in beside the G.I.

I am more alarmed than before! There is just one American soldier in the trench, and he is dead!

Where have the others gone? Could they all be killed or captured? The only other place they might have gone is to a farmhouse that is just across another field. Cautiously, ready to drop to the ground at any sound, I walk toward it. As I draw near my fear gets the better of me and I lie down behind a mound to study the situation.

There is no sign of life at the windows, but someone has crawled out of a low basement window and is crawling toward me.

"Over here!" a voice shouts.

A G.I. sits up and waves to me. I crawl over to him, and together we crawl back through the basement window. Inside there are a dozen men from my company and they have a captured Kraut. Everyone is sitting on the floor waiting for the rest of the company to assemble, and the Kraut is sitting on the floor with them.

He is ir his late twenties and looks like a veteran fighter. As he sees me studying him he takes out some pictures and hands them to me.

"My wife and children," he says in good English.

I know why he is doing this. I, too, would be nervous if I were alone in the hands of the enemy.

He continues speaking and is more talkative than most prisoners.

"You should not be fighting us," he says. "You are wrong to fight us."

"Why are you fighting?" I ask him.

"To keep communism out of Europe," he answers. Then he adds, "The Italians are not your friends. They are the worst. They will betray anyone. They were not loyal to us and will not be loyal to you. "

"Why did you surrender?" I ask him.

"I know the war is lost," he answers.

Shells begin to land very close to the house, so we look around for the best shelter. There is a connecting passageway that leads to another house, and this is farther away from the falling shells. We wait there for the rest of the company, and it is a long wait before everyone is together again.

We don't stay in the house, but move out along the road, advancing until we come to a small church. This provides more protection from the shells since the walls are very thick adobe; although the inside walls, which are pink plaster, are scarred from shrapnel- The furnishings are scattered all around.

Martin is feeling sick and the medics send him back to the hospital. Denny tells us he is leaving also, but his news is good news. He is being sent to the rear to receive a battle field promotion. He will be coming back as an officer, a second lieutenant.

For our sake I hope he will return soon. There are few experienced men left. The company is understrength and full of replacements.

Lieutenant James suddenly appoints me a squad leader. Marty and Martin are in the hospital and the many casualties have reduced our ranks until the company has only half the number needed. With all the new men I am already considered an experienced veteran.

My squad is thirteen men. I know nothing about them, and have just now learned their names. Until now they were just nameless G.I.s like so many others who come and go as faceless shadows in the night. Gathered around me is a group of strangers, but this doesn't matter. Combat is impersonal and at the front, although we work together as a unit, basically each man must depend upon himself. Orders are received and passed down. We follow along doing what is expected of us.

For the first time I am included in the briefing session before an attack. I follow Lieutenant James into the farmhouse, pushing aside the army blanket hung in the doorway to block any light. Inside, we form a ring around Captain Mathews, and the light from the candle casts just enough light for us to follow his finger as he traces the plan of attack on the map.

Our objective is another farmhouse about eight hundred yards from our present position. According to G-2 there are some Krauts dug in around the building and they are armed with machine guns. Our plan is to move across the flat fields in the dark and take up positions along the slope of the hill just below the house. At dawn we will begin firing.

There are only two officers in the company, Captain Mathews and Lieutenant James. I am glad to hear that Lieutenant James will be leading the attack. Having been a sergeant who won his commission in the field, he is battle wise.

As the briefing ends, Captain Mathews looks up at the ring of men around him, their faces shaded by their heavy helmets.

"Synchronize your watches. It is now 0242. We will leave at 0500. "

We rejoin the men who are waiting outside, scattered around the walled courtyard. Some lie on the ground, but most are sitting with their backs resting against the white plaster walls. There is time for sleep, but few feel like it.

Some of the men have not been in battle before, and they face it silently with the fear of the unknown. All of us dread the coming of 0500. Many thoughts will go through our minds before the order comes to move out.

The Krauts are nervous too, occasionally firing a machine gun our way. We watch the tracers, like strings of red beads in the night, and we pay little attention when a few stray bullets nick the other side of the house.

The starlight gives the white walls a ghostly, unreal look like a painting that lacks detail. The groups of men form dark mounds against the white background. I watch the mountain fog drift closer. Like misty hands it reaches over the wall and slides into the courtyard.

The time is passing slowly, but the dreaded hour is approaching. Battle time is not like other time, and it has little meaning. Our lives are measured by long periods of waiting followed by short seconds packed with fiery action. At last a voice in the night breaks the silence.

"It's 0500 men. Prepare to move out."

Struggling to our feet we buckle on our equipment. Then, like a serpent uncoiling, the single column flows out of the courtyard and stretches into the field.

The Germans have quit firing. The silence, the persistant fog and the darkness give us a sense of security. In my mind the white fog is a protective wall that surrounds me and hides me from the enemy. We have orders to maintain total silence, so our advance is like moving in a dream.

On and on we walk. Is it possible to take so long to go eight hundred yards? It is difficult to judge distance in the fog, but as we continue to advance I am growing nervous and uneasy.

Scraping sounds break the silence. Then German voices are loud and clear. The words are leaping out of the fog! Very close !

Simultaneously, like one long animal, the line freezes.

There is another German voice. Two soldiers are talking and digging a trench.

Lieutenant James moves back along the line motioning with his hand for everyone to lie down. We do this without a sound.

The lieutenant motions for the radio man to follow him to the rear of the line. The rest of us wait silently listening to the Kraut voices. The darkness and fog are our concealment, but it is growing lighter. At last a whispered order comes down the line telling us to withdraw. Quietly the rope of men pulls back.

When we are far enough back to speak in safety Lieutenant James tells us that he contacted Captain Mathews on the radio and explained that we were lost. Captain Mathews is coming out to find us and lead us to the objective.

How can the captain find us in the fog when there are no landmarks to be seen? We can't call out or make any noise that could lead him to us. It seems a dangerous and impossible mission.

Daylight is coming fast. We can see at least five yards through the thinning fog. Our danger is mounting.

"I don't know where the hell we are," Lieutenant James says. "There was supposed to be a hill, but we never came to one. We may have bi-passed it and got behind the Jerries. The house is on the hill."

We continue to retrace our steps. A series of explosions tear at the earth near us. We all dive to the earth and smell the acrid smell of mortar shells mixing with the fog.

We continue to pull back and there are no more shells. It seems doubtful the Krauts have detected us. The mortars are part of their scare tactics, like the occasional firing of machine guns.

Dawn is very near. The sky is turning to an ashen gray.

"Look! Jerries!" someone shouts.

Three Jerries are running toward us. We start to drop, but wait when we see their hands are in the air. They are yelling something, but none of us understands.

"Wait!" Malik says. "They're Polish."

Malik walks over to the Poles and they are all talking rapidly and laughing. The three grab each other around the neck and kiss each other. They would kiss Malik too, but he steps back.

"They're Poles and the Germans forced them to fight," he says, smiling.

They are still all dancing and patting each other. This wild jubilation makes us all smile.

"They put one Pole with ten Germans," Malik says. "If they don't fight they will kill them."

In the midst of all the confusion there is an apparition materializing in the fog. It is a miracle! It is Captain Mathews.

There is no time to waste. Our peril is growing greater by the minute with the morning light. Captain Mathews and Lieutenant James study the map and agree on a new direction. Once again the column starts to move forward.

It takes only a few minutes to reach the hill, and it turns out to be a very small hill. It is level on the top and there is the farmhouse and the Krauts.

As our company spreads out just below the crest of the hill, the Germans begin firing their machine guns. We are below their line of fire so the bullets are going over our heads and landing in the fields to our rear. We can't see the Krauts because there is a lot of shrubbery near the top of the hill. The bushes and small trees are especially thick along the crest, making a barrier between us. Only about sixty yards are separating the two armies.

Our men begin firing back at the Krauts, although we can't see them. They seem to be dug in all around the house and have plenty of fire power using both rifles and machine guns.

A man in my squad is crawling up the slope to see if he can spot the Krauts through the brush. I am right behind him, and suddenly I hear a loud metalic bang. The man drops back, lifts off his helmet and looks at the large holes in it. A bullet passed clear through it, grazing his scalp.

"I'm glad I'm not an inch taller," he says.

Besides our riflemen we have two automatic rifle teams and a thirty caliber machine gun, but the machine gunners are reluctant to fire too much from one position for fear of being spotted. The gun can't fire very long at one time because it is a heavy water cooled machine gun and the barrel heats up quickly.

The Krauts have a number of machine guns and a lot of riflemen. It is obvious we are well outnumbered, and they are well dug in. How can we take the position?

We bring maximum fire power on them hoping to terrorize them or cause them to panic, but it doesn't work. They just increase their own firing.

We have kept the fire fight going all morning and it is noon with still no break in the action. We try throwing hand grenades, but the Krauts respond by flipping their potato masher grenades at us. These make a whirring noise as they flip end over end, but they hit the trees and none of them reach our positions. Some of our grenades hit the trees too and when several bounce back we stop throwing them.

We have rifle grenades that we can fire off the ends of our rifles like small mortars. These have a greater range and with them we drive the Krauts back to their holes.

We have to cut down on our firing because we are running low on ammunition. The machine gun is especially low. We don't know what to do next and wonder if the Krauts will try to come after us. They must realize they outnumber us. We will certainly need our ammo if they decide to come.

We have a volunteer. A man in the company offers to try to go back across the field and get more ammo. It seems almost an impossibility for anyone to get across the flat area to the rear. It is bright daylight and the fog is gone completely.

Lieutenant James agrees to let the man try, and we all open fire on the Krauts to divert their attention and make them think we are going to attack.

The volunteer takes off running, keeping close to the ground and zig-zagging through the field. He only gets about ten yards before he is shot and pitches forward dead.

Lieutenant James orders light firing to conserve ammo. The Krauts give no indication of running low and they keep their machine guns ripping.

A G.I. comes over to Lieutenant James with an idea.

"I speak German. Let me talk with them under a flag of truce. Maybe I can talk them into surrendering."

"How are you going to do this?" he asks.

"I'll put up a white handkerchief and yell to them that I want to talk."

"You can talk to them," Lieutenant James says, "but you can't wave a white flag. They'll think we are surrendering."

"O.K.," the G.I. agrees. "Have everyone stop firing."

Lieutenant James orders a cease fire and the G.I. yells in German, asking them to hold their fire so we can talk.

Amazingly all the firing stops and there is complete silence.

Continuing to speak German, the G.I. tells them he is going to stand up so they can see him and he asks them to hold all fire while he talks to them.

A Kraut calls back and agrees to this.

We are all holding our breaths as we watch the American walk up to the crest of the hill and stand up. Two others lift him up on their shoulders so he can see better.

He tells the Germans that they will be treated well and be given safe conduct to the rear if they surrender. It is senseless for them to go on fighting when the war is lost. If the battle continues many people on both sides will be killed.

The German answer comes immediately and we listen to the translation. They must refuse our offer. It is we who should surrender. Our position is hopeless.

"Nein," the American replies and jumps down to the ground.

The shooting begins again, but the Krauts have brought up another weapon. There is a blast just behind us and a ring of smoke shoots into the air.

We all know what it is. The Krauts have fired a mortar and the first shot was a smoke round to mark the spot where it hit.

There is another explosion and another wisp of smoke curls upward. This one is closer. The third round hits just a few yards away. The Krauts have made the necessary corrections and are ready to begin the barrage. The hill will give us no protection. With the mortars they can devastate our entire line and we will have no place to go to escape.

Mortar shells go straight up and come almost straight down. A hill offers no shelter. "The Krauts can put a mortar shell in your hip pocket," is a common saying.

Quickly Lieutenant James calls the squad leaders together.

"You can see what's happening. In a few minutes they'll hit us with a mortar barrage that could wipe us out. If we try to pull back—well, you saw what happened to the man who went for ammo. The Krauts outnumber us maybe two to one, and they're dug in. I won't order an attack under these conditions. I want the squad leaders to decide on the action. If anyone has any suggestions we'll vote."

Carter, a small blond sergeant from the second platoon is the first to speak. He has been with the company all through the war and is battle wise.

"I vote to attack," he says. "It's suicide to try to pull back. They'll tear us to pieces if we stay here. We might as well go forward and take our chances."

The next squad leader nods. "Attack," he says.

Every squad leader votes to attack. When it is my turn I vote with the others. I would rather be shot in the front than the back, and I remember what the mortars did to Rule. There seems no other choice than to go forward. There are six unanimous votes.

"O.K.," Lieutenant James agrees. "Get your squads ready. When I drop my hand we'll go.

I explain the decision to the men in my squad and there are no objections. What are these inexperienced men thinking? Do they understand what they are being asked to do? They must know all the choices are deadly. No one wants to stay here and be blown to bits by mortars. There is no discussion at all. Some silently nod as if moved by destiny.

"Try to get into the house," I tell them. "Out in the open is the worst place to be because the Krauts are dug in. If you can get into the house you'll have some cover."

Our eyes are on Lieutenant James, and when his hand drops we jump up firing and racing over the crest of the hill at full speed. Crashing through the brush and into the flat yard, everyone is firing and yelling. It is bedlem! Insane confusion! We are moving as if hypnotized.

The noise is shattering! Guns are firing from all directions. Grenades explode! There is screaming!

We are running through a Fourth of July display, but I do not see what is happening around me. My eyes are glued on the basement windows of the house. There is no gunfire coming from there.

Beside me are two replacements from my squad, Bates and Kramer, and the three of us together leap feet first through the low windows and drop down to the dirt floor. Our guns are in the firing position but we find no one in the room.

The basement is a stable, but all the cows have been removed from the stalls and the straw scattered around. We search carefully through the hay but find no one. The back door is open.

"Let's move upstairs," I tell my buddies.

To do this we must go out in back and up an open stairway that leads to the second floor. When we start across the yard I see someone waving a white flag from a third story window.

We hear mortar shells coming in and I dive for the ground. There are a series of blasts around me. I have fallen beside a wounded Kraut. He is lying on his back and part of his side is blown away. He is silently blinking his eyes. We both know he is finished, and as I stare at his pale face a pig comes over and pushes its snout into the dying Kraut's mouth.

I look at the neat uniform with its medals and all I think of is the degredation. Where is the glory now? What a way to go! Mankind is insane!

Leaping up I run toward the stairs, but another shell forces me to hit the ground again. This time I am near a shed and a lamb comes over and stands beside me. Its throat is hanging open, red and torn. The lamb looks at me with pleading eyes.

I close my eyes and turn my head, then jump up and run again. When I get up to the second floor I find a number of G.I.s are already there. Continuing on, I race up the inside stairs to the third floor and look for the room where I saw a white flag.

The door to one of the rooms is locked and inside there are people banging the door and calling out. Since the key is still in the lock, I turn it and carefully push the door open. The room is full--at least fifty men, women and children are crowded together. When they see me they stare silently with apprehensive faces.

Seeing the fright in their eyes, I tell them the first words I can think of. It is poor Italian.

"Tu liberate."

The room erupts with loud cheers and clapping. Surging forward, the civilians engulf me with hugs and kisses. Other G.I.s have just come up to the third floor and the Italians are grabbing them and hugging them also.

A man tells me that the Germans had rounded up all the civilians and locked them in the room. They have been there for two days without food or water.

When the G.I.s hear this they pull out their K rations and break them open, offering the food to the women and children.

"Mangarie," we are saying, pressing the biscuits and tins of food into their hands.

Some of the civilians have tears in their eyes as they accept the offering.

From the window we can see some of the Krauts fleeing over the hill to the rear. Lieutenant James grabs the radio and calls for artillary, but is told the artillary is already firing on targets with a higher priority.

Out in front more than forty Krauts were surrounded and have surrendered. They. are marched around the house and placed in a store room next to the stable.

We have achieved our objective, but the price has been high. Half the company is dead or wounded. Of our squad of thirteen men only three of us remain, Bates, Kramer and me.

Lieutenant James is talking with Captain Mathews on the radio. They both agree that we have earned some rest, and plan to have us spend the night at the farm. We stretch out on the floor, suddenly realizing how tired we are. The civilians have slipped quietly away, but three have remained behind.

They tell us that they stayed to fix us something to eat. Somewhere they have found some eggs, and they make fried bread to go with them. Everything tastes good. Our senses are keen!

Some of us go outside for rations. The wounded who have gone to the aid station left their bed rolls and equipment on the ground. I find two K rations to replace those I have given away. I again come across the wounded Kraut with the hole in his side. He is finally dead.

Looking around in the house, I hardly know any of the men who are with me. It doesn't matter, they are all G.I.s. No one knows anyone anymore.

Blond Sergeant Carter is still with us and he is becoming one of our main leaders. Lieutenant James is here also. We are lucky. They are both capable and fair.

Captain Mathews arrives and praises us.

"Any men who did what you men did deserves a night's rest," he says. "And I'll try to get it for you."

Although he tries, he is soon over ruled by the battalion commander. The orders come through by radio for us to move out immediately and pursue the fleeing enemy.

Lieutenant James comes to me and gives me a different assignment. Since there are only three men left in my squad, we will stay behind to guard the prisoners until someone is sent up from the rear to take them back.

Taking over my new responsibility, I walk around the building to check the room where the prisoners are being held. It is just one story high and has been built on the back of the stable. There is one door that opens out into the yard, and on the opposite side there is a high window.

Since there are three of us, I decide that two of us will stand guard while the third one rests. We will rotate the posts every two hours. One man will stand outside the door and the other guard outside the window.

For the first assignment I put Bates at the window and I take the door post. Kramer will rest.

It is mid afternoon and the sun feels warm and good. I am enjoying it, leaning against the wall by the door. Suddenly I am hurled to the ground!

There are four rapid explosions! The door comes flying off and acrid smoke is pouring out of the room. With loud screaming and stamping, the prisoners are thundering out of the room like stampeding cattle.

Instantly I know what has happened! Some shells have made a direct hit on the room with the prisoners.

Leaping to my feet and aiming my rifle at them I order them to halt—but it is useless. They are yelling and hear nothing. They continue charging out in panic.

"In there!" I yell, pointing to the basement door.

The herd tramples and shoves down the ramp into the stable.

Bates comes stumbling around the shed holding his arm.

"I'm hit in the arm."

It is a minor wound by shrapnel, but the painful gash will need a bandage. I tell him to hurry into the stable to help Kramer guard the prisoners. Then, looking into the devastated shed I see the massive destruction.

Four heavy German mortars must have hit the roof, blowing it apart. Thatching, tile and timbers are littering the room. Where the ceiling should be there is blue sky, and on the floor are a number of German bodies.

Quickly I return to the stable where the prisoners have gathered together in one of the stalls. Kramer is standing guard. The Krauts are huddled together in fear and some of them are bleeding. Several appear to have serious wounds.

"Does anyone speak English?" I ask them.

"Yes," answers a tall prisoner. His uniform is dark rather than gray like the others.

"Are you an officer?"

"A captain," he answers.

"And these are your men?"

"Yes."

I ask the captain to come over into another stall. It seems safer to separate the officer from his men.

"Do you have first aid packets like these?" I ask him, showing him the pack we carry on our belts.

"No. We have no supplies."

"We have no extra ones," I tell him. "Do you have a medic with you?"

"Jerry," he calls out, and a prisoner steps forward. "He is a medic."

"Tell him to do what he can for the wounded," I tell him.

Then, turning to Kramer, I tell him that I am going back into the shed to see if any of the wounded there are still alive.

When I enter the room again I study the eleven bodies lying among the debris. As I am watching, one of the Krauts moves an arm. He looks badly wounded.

"Maybe it would be better to just let him die," I think to myself. Then I shake my head. "I can't play God."

Returning to the basement, I tell the captain that some of his men are still alive and I ask him to choose two men to go to the shed and carry back any who are wounded.

Quickly he barks out a command and two men jump up and go out. Soon they return carrying a wounded man. They make four trips and lay four seriously injured Krauts on the floor of the stable.

Jerry, the medic, checks these wounded men. They are moaning and one is calling for water.

Strangely, an Italian man appears with a bucket of water. Handing it to me, he scowls at the German captain.

"It is for you," he says. "But not for them!" he adds emphatically.

"Grazie," I tell him. "Where did you get it?"

He says something that I take to mean there is a well, and he points to the yard. Then he quickly leaves, for the shells are beginning to fall around the house.

"Your wounded need water," I tell the captain. "You may send one man out to the well to get water."

Again the captain gives a sharp command and a German soldier leaps forward. He takes one of the buckets in the stable and goes out among the shells and brings back water from the well.

When he returns, we give the water to Jerry to distribute to the wounded.

It has grown dark outside and the shells are still falling around the house. The room has taken on the appearance of a hospital ward with wounded lying around on the floor. The seriously injured are feverish and they keep calling out for "vaser" and for "Jerry."

Bates is in great pain because of his arm, so Kramer and I plan to trade off watching the prisoners while he rests on the hay. We have taken over one of the stalls for our own. From this stall we can look directly across at the German captain and can also see, at an angle, into the stall that holds the rest of the prisoners.

With the coming of night we light candles. It is risky to do this in a room with windows, but it would be more dangerous to not be able to see the Krauts.

Kramer is standing in the middle of the room with his rifle in front of him at port arms and I am reclining on the hay with Bates when suddenly a shot rings out.

The Krauts are on their feet and someone cries out.

Bates and I are both up with our rifles in front of us.

"My gun went off," Kramer says. "I don't know how it happened. I guess I touched the trigger."

Seeing the near panic among the prisoners, I turn to the captain.

"Tell your men it was an accident. His gun went off accidentally."

The captain cooperates and passes on the message. Some of the prisoners are talking to him with excited voices.

"One of the men was hit," the captain explains.

Going over to where the prisoners are sitting in the hay, I ask who has been shot. A young soldier who looks about sixteen stands up.

"Where were you hit?" I ask. The captain repeats my question in German.

The young Kraut puts both hands on his upper leg and when I beckon him forward he limps out to where I am standing. I examine the wound and see that it is a flesh wound. The bullet passed cleanly through and no bone was hit.

"It is just a flesh wound," I tell the captain, and he translates for me. "It is not serious."

I motion for the wounded man to go back with the others, and he sits down in the hay. His young, frightened face is still pale.

Outside it is beginning to rain and we listen to it hitting against the windows. The prisoners have grown quiet, but no one is sleeping. The loud moaning of the wounded men is the only noise

"Vaser. Vaser," someone is calling out.

"Jerry," another calls.

The hours of the night pass slowly, until near midnight there is a noise at the door and Sergeant Carter come in with two other G.I.s. They are all soaked and muddy.

"The Krauts counter attacked," Carter says. "It was pitch black and they were firing all around us. They got closer and closer and began throwing hand grenades. We were surrounded and one Kraut was close enough to see my stripes because he called out 'You better surrender Sergeant.'"

The three G.I.s sit down around the candle as if it is a fire and can warm them.

"The captain disbanded the company," Carter continues. "He told everyone to try to make it back to the farmhouse on his own. They should all be coming here. We're the first I guess. I don't know how we got through the Krauts."

All through the early hours of the morning men are trickling back to the farmhouse. A few at a time they arrive. Captain Mathews and Lieutenant James come in also.

By morning all the men that are left in the company have assembled and Captain Mathews radios for reinforcements to support us. The answer he gets is that there are none available. We are ordered to withdraw and take all the prisoners with us who can walk.

In the morning sunlight we walk single file back across the flat fields to the other farmhouse, the one from which we launched our attack twenty-four hours earlier.

The prisoners, with their hands resting on their heads, walk along with us. Behind, on the floor of the basement, are over a dozen Krauts too seriously injured to walk. What will become of them we don't know.

During the day a detail arrives from the rear to take the prisoners off our hands. Also, more replacements arrive and we are ordered to walk to another sector to join the rest of the battalion.

The Kraut captain pays us a complement. He praises our company and says he would have been proud to command such a unit.

Through the rainy nights we go
On terrain we do not know
While the lightning
Is bouncing from cloud to cloud
With thunder loud
A repetitious scene
That's endless

NINETEEN

There is no definite front. The lines are fluid with both sides moving among the mountains like guerrilla bands, attacking one objective after another. Yet, we push steadily north and the Krauts fall back to their prepared positions, harassing us with artillery, machine guns, mortars and sniper fire. We face the additional hazard of mines, mines conceived by cunning minds. Like the Italian box mine that shoots two feet into the air before exploding, so the shrapnel will fly out in all directions. They are devices to kill or castrate a man.

Tanks, also, appear unexpectedly. We listen to the roar of their motors and clanking of their treads in the night. When they find us they shell our positions with their powerful eighty-eights,

It is important to keep moving and to keep our positions hidden. We rarely stop in one place for long, digging slit trenches and moving two or three times a day. During the day we have British air support and we watch the daring pilots with their spitfires diving right down to machine gun the anti-aircraft guns that are shooting at them. When a plane is hit and the pilot is floating down in his parachute, we send out a patrol. There are plenty of volunteers for these rescue patrols as we try to reach the pilot before the Krauts capture him. It is a race in which we are often successful.

We have been strengthened by the return of some of our veteran men. Denny is back with his second lieutenant bars, and Marty was released from the hospital after treatment for venereal disease.

"That's what they put on my record," he tells us.

We are surprised to see Wallace back with our platoon. It is unfair that he should be sent back into action when he is deaf in one ear. His head wound destroyed his hearing so he can't hear anyone talking to him from the left side. I can't believe there is a shortage of healthy men in the rear areas!

I am back in Marty's squad, along with Ayers, Malik, Davis and Martin. The rest are replacements.

To cut down the Krauts' visual advantage, we now advance at night by artificial moonlight. The great batteries of searchlights are mounted along the ridge to the rear where they can bounce light off the clouds.

"We advance at night so the Krauts can't see us, then we make moonlight to light up the landscape so we can see where we're going. Does it make sense?" Ayers asks.

The artificial moonlight is noticeable when the weather is cloudy but dry. When it is raining the mountains are in total darkness.

A steady drizzle is falling as we cross one ridge and continue on toward the next one. Far in the distance there is a burning building that flickers and flashes like a spot of flame on a black background. Tonight it is the only light in our hell It seems to be an unreal image that holds our eyes and draws us toward it like moths to a flame.

The house is miles away and we think it will be burned to the ground long before we reach it. Hours later, as we are drawing near to it, the building is burning with that same steady flame. The flickering light in the windows is hypnotic and almost peaceful, like the burning logs of a fireplace on a wet, cold night.

Booming explosions shatter the night! The ground quivers and choking smoke is all around us. We clutch at the earth, but there is no protection in the plowed field. The shrapnel is singing and screeching as it sails around us.

"Run forward!" Captain Mathews calls out.

Jumping up, we all race around the hill to get away from the shell fire. We have escaped the barrage, but we are on the wrong side of the hill. It will soon be morning and we will be in full sight of the enemy.

As the shelling lets up, we reluctantly pull back to the place where we were hit. Our officers have decided to advance no farther until they know more about the enemy's location and strength. They order us to dig in and camouflage the trenches.

The drizzle has turned to rain and the soil is clay. Every time I drive the shovel into the earth the soggy soil sucks at it, hugging it tight, so that I can only pull it out by twisting the handle and working it back and forth.. When I finally pry the shovel loose, the earth releases it with spitting and hissing.

We are getting anxious knowing the Krauts have the spot zeroed in for artillery, but digging trenches is impossible. In desperation we turn to our hands, clawing out the soil with our fingers. Scratching, patting and molding the clay, we build walls around us.

What have we accomplished? We spend the rest of the night in clay bathtubs. It is miserable, but we are lucky! The night has remained guiet.

Our officers are taking advantage of the light from the burning house, gathered together studying the maps.

A lone shell whistles in. The roof of the building flies to pieces with a massive blastl It is over in a split second, but all of our officers are wounded!

Captain Mathews and Lieutenants James and Denny are all treated by the medics. All three are taken to the aid station.

"They're going to the hospital," Allen tells us.

All at once! The three who led charmed lives! Even Denny who seemed to have a protecting wall around him! The odds catch up with everyone. Do any of us really have much chance?

The morning light shows us a farmhouse on the next hill, just below us. We are in the direct line of sight and if it is occupied by the Krauts we may be under observation. We hope our muddy walls will hide us. Certainly our uniforms won't give us away, for they are the color of the clay.

A series of booms echo through the mountains and pieces of the roof fly off the house. Our artillery is firing on the building.

The door facing us flies open and seven Krauts rush out screaming with panic.

"Don't shoot at them," Sergeant Carter warns us. "Don't give our position away if you don't want to catch hell from the artillery."

Still yelling, the enemy run around the house, down the hill and disappear among the trees in the ravine.

All day we sit like drowned eagles in high muddy nests, waiting for orders and darkness before advancing again. Battalion headquarters sends us a new CO.--a second lieutenant. With the coming of night, led by an inexperienced officer, Lieutenant Mitchel, we move forward again.

It is a long night march to another sector. By morning we are following a road that is deep with mud. One that crosses a winding river back and forth, every few miles. All the stone bridges have been blasted by the retreating Germans and we have to wade into the icy water and pull each other up over the broken stones that were the foundation supports for the bridges.

Some tank destroyers are moving along the road with us, their steel turrets heavily camouflaged with branches. When our communications jeep rolls by, we all yell at the two linemen and hold up our thumbs. They are lucky. They get to ride.

An hour later we see the jeep again, only now it is black and twisted. It has hit a mine.

Before leaving the road to follow a trail back into the mountains, we all fill our canteens in the river, for in spite of all the rain drinking water is still a constant problem.

As we climb the slippery, muddy trail my legs will not keep up. They ache and are weak. My will power can't keep my body moving and I am falling behind. I wonder if the diarhea has weakened me. It is not until the company stops to dig in that I am able to close the gap. Joining a new replacement, I do my digging on my knees.

Exhausted, I fall into a deep sleep for several hours. In the morning we start up the trail again, but my legs are better and I am able to stay with the squad.

Suddenly an explosion! We hit the ground, but it is just one stray shell. A new man who joined the company yesterday is hit. The medics work over him, but he turns a sickly yellow and is dead. How quickly life goes! None of us knew him. He had just one day of action.

When we near the rocky summit we step to dig trenches again. I try working with Ayers, but it is no good. He is nervous and can't stay still, refusing to use the hole after we have finished. Again he leaves me there alone. Without emotion I watch him go.

I think I am becoming more fatalistic. Whatever is meant to happen will happen! Yet, I still believe in being cautious. Like Marty and Martin I am trying to be careful and take few chances.

One man in our platoon, Thomas, is an absolute fatalist. He never digs a slit trench and sits on top of the ground during a barrage. One time a piece of shrapnel ripped off the side of his helmet, but it didn't touch him. This only confirmed his belief that it doesn't matter what you do you will die when it is your time. He continues to lead a charmed life.

With an inexperienced CO. our position is more hazardous. Such a person can jeapordize our lives and put us in real peril.

It is near midnight on a very dark night when Lieutenant Mitchel comes to my hole and asks me to go with him to check on the machine gun outposts around the area. Sergeant Carter is with him and the three of us start out walking toward the outposts It is a risky thing to do when it is so dark we can hardly see each other, and I don't remember anyone attempting such a check in the middle of the night before.

"How do we know the men on the outposts won't mistake us for the enemy?" I ask.

"Come on," Lieutenant Michel says, ignoring my question.

Nervously, at a fast pace we follow him down the hill, but we find no machine guns.

"They're out here somewhere," Lieutenant Mitchel says.

"They wouldn't be this far away," Carter cautions him.

"They must be over here," the lieutenant insists, starting off again.

"I think we're way beyond them," Carter says, stopping. "You're heading into the Kraut lines."

"No, I'm sure they're out here," Lieutenant Mitchel continues

"I'm not going any farther in that direction," Carter says.

"You're heading into the German lines."

"What do you think?" the lieutenant stops and turns to me.

"I think we've gone too far. The outposts should be closer to the company positions." Like Carter, I have grave doubts about the location of the guns, and I have confidence in Carter's experience.

"Go back then!" Lieutenant Mitchel snaps. Spinning on his heels he takes off again.

Carter and I watch him disappear in the night heading toward the Germans. Cautiously we pick our way back up the hill and find our holes.

"We may never see him again," Carter says.

An hour later, when we hear someone trudging up the hill we stare into the darkness with our rifles ready. Carter's prophecy is wrong, for it is Lieutenant Mitchel who stomps by our slit trenches without saying a word.

Time is blurred by the frequent rain showers, and the days and nights seem to run together. We have no news, only rumors. We are to be relieved by the Eighty-fifth. We will be relieved tomorrow by the British. Sometimes the radio man tunes in to Axis Sally, but of course her reports are for propaganda purposes.

"She says we're crazy for throwing away our gas masks," he tells us. "We'll regret it soon."

It is true we no longer carry the bulky piece of equipment, but she doesn't worry us. If the Krauts violate the Geneva convention and use gas, we feel certain they will get the worst of it.

Axis Sally also calls the men of our division killers and claims we kill prisoners. She compares us to the Eighty-fifth, calling them gentlemen.

"Where can I get an Eighty-fifth shoulder patch?" Marty asks. "In case I get captured."

The ground is often littered with leaflets--Kraut propaganda. There is one that is the picture of a fat man with his hand on the leg of a pretty girl. The message warns us that the Jews at home are seducing our wives and girl friends while we fight. Another leaflet tells of the super weapons the Germans are developing. With these they will win the war.

A picture of the German luxury liner Europa appears on the front of one of the leaflets. We are offered a safe passage home on this ship if we surrender.

Many of us do not have combat boots or field jackets and the weather is cold and wet. The Krauts make the most of this in one of their propaganda papers, telling us that the reason we are so poorly equipped is because of the war profiteers at home.

Finally we get the field jackets and the bed rolls we've been needing. The bed rolls are mummy style sleeping bags that we tie with a rope and sling over our shoulders. When we stop to rest now it is real luxury to crawl into the warm bag and feel the softness, but we're afraid to take off our helmets or shoes and we sleep with a side unzipped so our hands are free to grab our rifles.

At times someone will crouch down in the bottom of his slit trench and set fire to his small ration box. For a few minutes there is some heat to warm the hands or take the chill off a cup of coffee, but most of the time we are afraid to create the little bit of smoke. We just eat everything cold.

Replacements continue to come and die--nameless faces. To escape the daily repetition of tension and misery, I begin to read. If it is daylight and we are pinned down in our slit trenches by mortar fire I read one of the two books I carry with me, The New Testament or the Pocket Book of Verse. When I find a copy of "Botany Bay" among the supplies it is like finding treasure. It is an Armed Forces Edition, a small paper back, so I can slip it inside my shirt.

My wallet has the pictures of my family in it, but they are welded to the leather by the constant soaking. Also in my wallet are three four leaf clovers that I found at the replacement depot at Caserta. I tell myself they are only souveniers from those green fields, not good luck charms.

The razor in my shirt pocket is rusty and rarely used.

With so many new replacements in the company, the veterans are drawing closer together. I talk frequently with the platoon guide, Sarvo. While we are eating our rations, sitting out on the ground, I look over at him and see him looking at the blue sky. A chill passes through me. In his face I see the same look I saw in Marty's. It is as if death is calling him to the beyond!

TWENTY

All signs indicate we are in for heavy action. An all night march has brought us to an assembly area where the entire battalion is waiting. Joining with the other companies is a surprise, for we were told nothing.

We have just arrived when Sarvo comes over to tell me that he and I have been chosen to go with A Company as it goes up Mt. Grande. Lieutenant Mitchel confirms the plan.

"A and B companies are going to lead the assault while our company will be the back up reserve. You and Sarvo will go with them and when they reach the objective you'll come back and lead our company to their positions."

We have to hurry, for A Company is already filing out of the area and starting up the mountain. Their .CO. has been anxious to get started while it is still dark, and he was only waiting for the arrival of our company. Sarvo and I fall in at the end of the line. B Company is forming to follow us.

I feel insecure about this assignment. Sarvo is the platoon guide, trained in this sort of thing, but I don't know what is expected.

As usual, it is an overcast night and I can hardly see the man ahead of me. To make it more confusing the trail keeps turning and twisting around the side of the mountain.

"Pop!" I dive for cover. The entire line is flat on the ground and frozen. Like a giant searchlight a parachute flare hangs in the sky illuminating the entire landscape. It is a full moon----three full moons!

At the same time a Kraut machine gun litters the mountainside with tracers. Nobody moves and we can't tell the location of the gun.

The flare disclosed some large boulders, so when it is finally dark again we all move over closer to them. The towering, massive walls of rock give the illusion of protection. There is no more firing from the Kraut gun.

Like a giant millipede crawling over sand and rock our line picks its way up the mountain. The darkness is alive and breathing. We are sensitive to it and know the enemy is there. We feel what we can't see.

When we stop again we have reached a small plateau and it is light enough to see a rectangular one story house squatting at the far edge as if ready to jump off toward the German side.

The men from A Company have spread out and they are advancing across the level area toward the house. Sarvo and I move with them.

The ground explodes! Fountains of live coals are erupting all around us! Instinctively we race for the cover of the house. The mortar shells are raining from the sky, driving us forward and filling our minds with the one mad thought that we must get off the level plain.

Tearing open a heavy wood door, we plunge into absolute darkness! We are blind! Not a ray of light penetrates the solid walls of the windowless room. There is the feel of straw underfoot suggesting a stable. Listen! We are not alone. Heavy breathing indicates there are a number of people in the room.

They are not G.I.s, for we were the first to reach the house. Are they Italian civilians, or German soldiers?

Sarvo is saying nothing. We are both frozen, listening. The people in the room are silent.

Taking a chance, and a deep breath I ask, "Quanta kilometer Tedeschi?"

An answer comes but I don't understand the words. Terrified, I whisper to Sarvo that I don't understand anything. It doesn't sound like Italian.

Quickly we back out the door. The mortar barrage has ended. Circling the house we find some G.I.s from A Company gathered near the front door. Their CO. is talking with his officers in the front room.

Sarvo and I slip inside and tell them about the people in the stable. The CO. says he will send someone to investigate.

The sky is growing brighter and neither Sarvo nor I want to go down the mountain in the daylight.

"Maybe we can spend the day here and go back when it gets dark," I suggest.

Sarvo thinks this is a good idea and wants to check out the attic to see if there is a good place to catch some sleep. We ask the CO. about doing this and he quickly shakes his head.

"NO! Go back right now! I want your company up here at once. There's no resistance now, but the Krauts know we're here and could attack at any time."

Starting down the trail, with Sarvo in the lead, we find it is much darker than we thought it would be. We still can't see any trail and all we can be sure of is we are going down hill.

Finally Sarvo stops and asks me if I know the way.

"I've no idea," I tell him. "I'm just following you. The trail turned so much coming up that I lost all sense of direction."

"Well, I'm lost," he admits. "You lead for a while."

We start off again with me running in front, but I have no idea where we are going.

Something is moving in the dim light ahead! A band of moving shadows is approaching. Sarvo sees it too and without a word we both drop behind some nearby rocks.

"What company are you from?" I shout.

With a noisy clatter all the figures drop to the ground.

I call out again, but there is no answer.

"Are you from C Company?" I ask.

"Yes," someone shouts.

For verification I shout out our names and ask theirs. Sarvo and I recognize a few of them; It is another miracle! We have stumbled into the company area.

Lieutenant Mitchel orders the company to move up at once. With Sarvo and me in the lead we start the climb up Mt. Grande.

"I still don't know where I'm going," I tell Sarvo. "There doesn't seem to be a trail. It's confusing as hell!"

"I don't know either," he admits. "I hope we end up in the right place."

It is growing lighter, but this is still no help to me. I couldn't see anything before so none of the landmarks look familiar to me. What has happened to the Kraut machine gun? We climb in silence, meeting no opposition.

Somehow we end our climb in just the right place. The men from A Company are gathered along the edge of the plateau and their CO. has decided to set up a command post in the house.

Two telephone linemen are walking toward the building holding a reel of wire between them. Step by step the approach the house letting the wire drop to the ground as they go.

"Whing!" One lineman drops to the ground with a cry.

We are all on the ground trying to figure out where the shot came from. There is a hay stack near the house and a sniper could be hiding there. It's also possible the Krauts have slipped back into the house. I am thinking of how Sarvo and I wanted to sleep in the attic.

A five man combat team from our company is moving across the plateau to rescue the fallen man. Like shadows they run and drop, pop up and dash forward again, moving closer to the lineman. We watch with our rifles ready to fire.

I watch with special interest and have empathy with the injured man. Lineman was my specialty in communications. That could be me. The medics have reached the fallen lineman and the combat team is searching around the hay stack. They find nothing.

"The sniper slipped back down the hill," Marty says. "G-2 says there's a village down there and the Krauts have turned it into a fort. That was the original objective, but it was changed.

Mortars are crashing down again! We are still on the ground and dirt and smoke are all around us. Great wounds are opening up all over the plateau.

The men to our rear leap over a small cliff to safety, but the rest of us are lying on our stomachs trying to scratch out some depressions with our shovels.

A Kraut machine gun opens fire across the plateau! Survival out in the open is impossible! Frantically I look for a way to escape.

There is a strip of scrub brush a few yards away and some of the men are crawling or rolling toward it. With instant recklessness I follow them.

Among the bushes I find a slight depression and I flatten myself into it. This saves me from the machine gun but offers no protection from the mortars and there is still a stretch of open ground between me and the security of the cliff.

"Over here! Run for it!" A sergeant is waving his arms and calling to us.

A G.I. jumps up and runs. The Kraut machine gun fires, but the man is over the cliff.

Another G.I. runs and the machine gun fires again. The man goes down, hit in the legs. The sergeant pulls him to safety.

"Run!" he is shouting to me. "It's your only chance!"

I wait a few seconds, counting to ten.

They are waving and yelling for me to come.

I wait a few seconds more. Then, with a pounding heart, I hurtle myself toward the cliff.

The machine gun fires—but too late! I tumble over the cliff and out into space. Several pairs of hands grab me and pull me down to a ledge. As the men jerk me back my bed roll goes over my head and bounces down into the canyon below. My morale is cascading down the mountain with it! The nights in the mountains are very cold now and there goes my only chance to keep warm!

There's no time to waste. I join with a new replacement and begin digging a slit trench on the ledge. Ayers and Marty are digging next to me, but suddenly Ayers stops digging and says it isn't safe. When he leaves, Allen joins Marty to finish the hole.

While we dig. the mortars scream past us like savage wolves escaping from their iron vaults. Our ledge is too narrow for them to touch us and they shriek as they crash into the canyon below.

The entire company is dug in along the ledge and the space is so scarce that Marty's hole is close enough for us to reach out and touch it. There's not enough room to dig a trench we can lie down in, so we go very deep. Sitting up we have over a foot of space above our heads.

Fortunately I still have my shelter half, so we have a cover to spread out and protect us from the light rain that is beginning to fall.

We are just finishing when Sarvo comes over and tells me that the battalion commander wants to come up to our positions.

"You're to go down and lead him up."

"Why me?" I ask suspiciously. "You're the platoon guide--the staff sergeant."

"You know the way."

"No better than you do! I think the CO. gave you the order and you're trying to pass the buck."

"I'm giving you an order," he says angrily. "Follow it or I'll have you court martialed when we go back."

"To hell with that! It's your job. Who told you to have me go?"

While we are: arguing we see a man with a walking stick striding up the hill like an English gentleman out for a stroll.

"There's the battalion commander now," Marty says.

"Why would he come up the mountain in broad daylight?" I ask. "We don't know where the Krauts are or if any area is secure. We're lucky to be hanging onto this ledge."

"Somehow he made it," Marty says. "You didn't think that was possible, did you Sarvo."

Sarvo turns and walks back to his hole, but I'm still angry.

"I still think the CO. asked him to lead the major up."

"It's his job," Marty agrees.

The Krauts are shelling us again, but the heavy artillery shells are passing over and taking huge bites out of the green turf on the hill below us.

It is evening and rain is falling from the heavy dark clouds. Bradford and I climb down into the slit trench and pull the shelter half across the top. The trench is crowded and we have to sit with our knees drawn up under our chins, but we are exhausted and it feels good just to be sitting down.

"Two days ago I was at a desk in North Africa," Bradford says. "I'm a clerk, not a rifleman."

"It doesn't matter," I tell him. "I was in communications. Everybody in the army can shoot a rifle. You just do what you have to and try to stay alive. When I joined the company I just watched Marty. He's been with the company since it was formed in the states. He and Sarvo have both managed to make it through without being wounded."

"They just came into the office and told me to get my things together," Bradford continues. "They stuck me on a plane and two days later here I am."

The rain is beating hard on the shelter half, but we are staying dry. I close my eyes. It has been twenty-four hours since I've had any sleep, but my mind is active. I think of my argument with Sarvo. Marty was on my side. The two are always rivals, both bucking for higher rank.

Somehow I drop off to sleep and out of the war. My mind succumbs to the fatigue of my body.

Deafening blasts shatter my sleep! The earth is heaving and churning! Giant feet are jumping on me! I can't move!

Suddenly it is clear. The shelterhalf is pressing down on me and the heaviness is dirt and rock. The canvas is forming a small pocket of air around my chin. I can breath, but I can't move. I try to raise my arms but it's impossible. My feet, too, are pinned down. I can move nothing!

With all my breath I yell for help. A chill of fear runs through me. My buddy is only inches away, but he isn't moving.

"Help!" I yell again.

My voice sounds muffled and far away. Can it be heard through all the mud and rock covering me? The shelling noises are continuing. We are in a barrage. No one will get out of his hole during a shelling.

I yell again, fearing we might smother before anyone discovers what has happened. Desperately I squirm, trying to move something, but it is in vain. I am pinned down tight. Buried alive!

The weight is growing lighter. Hands reach down and touch my head. The dirt and canvas are pulled away from my face. Wallace is digging frantically with his shovel and soon Bradford and I are able to pull ourselves out.

We are sitting in the mire assuring Wallace that neither of us is hurt, while the shells continue to bang into the cliff above us. There are cries from wounded men all along the line.

Wallace races off into the night to check on the moans. The shrapnel is thundering into the dirt and bouncing off the rocks with metalic cries and shrieks.

There is a lull in the shelling and Wallace returns. He is bleeding from a shrapnel wound to his arm, but he ignores it and goes on bandaging some wounded men.

Marty is found unconscious and the litter bearers carry him up to the aid station that is in the church on top of the hill. Although he is unconscious he fights with the medics and they have trouble keeping him on the stretcher.

Bradford and I are sitting in the mud as if we are in a stupor. We are watching the blue flashes of the artillery guns firing along a line to the rear. More shells are tearing into the cliff above us.

Suddenly the coils of fear crush the breath out of me as I realize I'm out in the open with no protection.

"How can the Krauts hit us?" I ask Bradford. "They're on the other side of the mountain and the shells are hitting the cliff on this side."

Ayers comes running down the line and drops beside me.

"It's our own artillery," he says. "See the flashes along the horizon. They're not clearing the mountain."

The truth of his statement hits me as I watch those blue flashes that light up the sky and see more shells tearing into the cliff.

"You're right!" I agree. "We've got to get it stopped."

"It's our own artillery!" Ayers yells. "Pass the word!"

"It's our own artillery!" the words echo and are repeated all along the line.

The shelling is increasing and strange noises are vibrating the air. There are buzzing and flapping sounds combined with the fiery showers of shrapnel.

"I've got to get back," Ayers says. "Shorty's been hit again. Third time. I moved him to my hole."

He takes off running, leaving Bradford and me crouching in the muddy ruins of our hole. Several shells come close and I duck into the mud as the ground quakes. Red shrapnel rips into my rations and equipment. I tremble and clutch for shelter.

Ayers comes running back to us.

"You're insane!" I shout. "Stop running around during a barrage!"

"Shorty was killed by that one," he says. "Come on! Let's find a radio."

What do I have to lose? I have no cover or shelter. Jumping up, I follow him down the line. Suddenly I realize that I am one of the crazy ones running around during a barrage.

Bradford follows me and the three of us slide and stagger around until we find Lieutenant Mitchell's canvas covered hole. The ground is shaking violently and my senses no longer seem to be functioning rationally. Each shell is creating more terror and panic.

In a chorus of voices we are all shouting at the CO.

"It's our own artillery. Call them on the radio! This is all from our own artillery!"

No head appears but a voice shouts back from under the shelter half.

"Don't tell me. What can I do?"

"Use the radio!" Ayers yells.

"There's nothing I can do."

"Hell!" Ayers yells. "Let's go to the major."

We are off again, racing and stumbling, trying to reach the church on top of the hill. I smash into bushes and small trees that tear at my clothes and knock me sideways. Grasping for support, I fall over some rubble. Beaten and bruised, I crawl to my feet and feel my way along a broken wall.

The three of us continue to grope along the wall of the church with our hands until we reach a doorway. It is just as dark inside the church. The room is packed with soldiers who are sandwiched together all over the floor. The entire building is rocking from the nearby explosions.

Ayers asks to see the major, but the CO. of A Company says we can't do that.

"I've got to see him," Ayers says. "This is our own artillery firing."

"You can see them firing all along the line," I add.

"You can't tell about that," the CO. says. "The Krauts fire at the same time we do. They're firing right now."

"This can't be Kraut artillery," the three of us insist. "The shells are hitting the cliff where we're dug in. We're on the opposite side of the mountain from the Krauts. It's impossible for Kraut artillery to hit there!"

We sound so certain and convincing that the CO. gives in and says one of us can go in and talk with the major. We tell Ayers to go.

The room is so full of men that Bradford and I can't move without stepping on someone, so we just sink down to the floor to wait. It is a long time before Ayers returns.

"The major wouldn't believe me ,at first," he says. I told him about the cliff and all the casualties. I had to tell the bastard a dozen times."

"Is he going to do anything?" Bradford asks.

"Yeh, he's calling them on the radio now."

All this talking has drawn attention to us and the CO. tells us in blunt language that we are not welcome to stay. He tells us to go back to our holes.

"We can't go back," I argue. "We don't have any holes. Our whole section is wiped out."

"It's too dangerous to be running around in a barrage," Ayers adds.

A compromise is reached. We can stay with A Company until morning if we will take a turn at outpost. We willingly agree to this. A Company is short of men, although it doesn't seem possible when the building is so packed.

I am the first to go on outpost and my station is a shattered corner room of the church. The walls are in ruins with rock scattered all around, and the roof is gone so it is open to the sky. Pieces of rubble and debris have been hurled out into the yard where they form eerie shapes in the dark. Sitting on the rubble, I wonder if it is possible to detect a Kraut patrol if one is out there.

The major must have contacted someone because the shelling is almost stopped. The first light of morning outlines two dead Krauts by the well.

We return to our own company area, but all we find is a sea of mud and a total disaster scene. Soroyan, a replacement in our squad, offers to share his hole with us. Bradford and I gratefully accept, but Ayers prefers to go his own way.

It is crowded with three of us in one slit trench, but the hole is very deep and we can all sit up easily.

Hoping to salvage some of my equipment, I go back to my former slit trench, but one look tells me it is an impossible job. The shelter half is riddled with shrapnel holes and half buried in the mud. It is difficult to tell where the hole was located, and the cliff above it is still falling down chunk by chunk, forming piles of clay and mud. The only thing I can recover is my shovel.

While I am digging around, Wallace comes over to talk to me. He says that Marty is dead. He never regained consciousness. The medics could only find a shrapnel wound in his leg. They think he died of shock or internal injuries.

I feel numb when I hear the news. Nothing shocks me any more.

"What chance do any of us have?" I ask Wallace. "Nobody was more careful than Marty. I patterned my combat behavior after him. Then he was killed by our own artillery."

Marty's light pack is sunk in the mud. In it he carried his few personal possessions and candy bars from the PX ration. Some of his stationary is in the water. His carbine, too, is on the ground still looking clean and well oiled. I don't touch anything.

We are forced to run for our holes when the Krauts unleash a savage attack with heavy mortars. All through the day and night the barrage continues. We are pinned down in our trenches, afraid to get out for any reason except to relieve ourselves.

The Krauts know exactly where we are and they pepper us with their "screaming meamies" constantly. These are their terror weapons, five barreled mortars that fire the salvo of five shots high into the air. As the shells fall back toward the earth they shriek and scream. The sound begins high in the sky as a faint cry. Then, as the shells draw nearer the screams get louder. They seem to be coming right down on top of you. Finally there are five loud blasts as they hit the earth, and you know they've missed you.

We are running low on rations. Whenever the Italian mountain troops try to bring us water or supplies their mule trains are shelled, and sometimes patrols will slip through to machine gun them. The trail is littered with dead Italians.

It is our third night on Mt. Grande and heavy machine guns have been brought up. We dig gun emplacements for them every five yards across the crest of the mountain. From now on we will take turns manning the guns day and night.

It is the first night the guns are in place and it is raining very hard. Once again our shelter halves cover all the slit trenches. They are still muddy from the previous rain and this causes confusion. Some bitter words echo through the dark.

"Hey, what the hell are you doing?"

"Damn! Why don't you watch where you're going?"

I am listening to the commotion outside as I sit warm and dry in our hole. Then Soroyan returns to the hole and tells me it is my turn to go up on outpost.

"Be careful," he warns me. "The guys are dug in all over and with the shelter halves over their holes you can't tell where they are. I fell on top of some guys and they were pretty sore."

Wearily I climb out and sink half way to my knees in the sloppy mud. My back aches and my legs are cramped from sitting for so long in the slit trench. My knees feel like they're out of joint.

I try to look around and find my bearings, but it is too dark to see any landmarks. I reel around, trying to establish a direction. If I go the wrong way I could fall down into the canyon. When I take two cautious steps forward my feet go out from under me.

"What the hell! Not again!"

A dim figure struggles out of the hole into which I am sliding.

"I hope you're not the same guy who fell in here a minute ago," he says.

"No," I mumble. "Sorry! You can't see anything out here and I'm trying to find my way to the outpost."

I help him clean out the hole and spread the shelter half over it again. We are both soaked before we are finished.

Still unable to see the ground, I start out again. Three steps later I go down over waste deep. Fortunately I have not fallen into the same hole, but from the cussing I get, it might as well have been.

I am as demoralized as the men I keep falling in on. It seems impossible to get up to the machine guns, but I have to keep trying. Then, when I do get there, I'll have to find my way back in two hours.

Cautiously I start forward again, and this time I make it all the way with no more accidents.

It is a lonely outpost that each man must stand by himself. No sooner have I taken over than the screaming meamies start coming in again. I have to keep my head up to keep a lookout, but all my impulses want me to duck down to avoid any shrapnel from the mortars.

In the night every shadow takes a human form and every click is the sound of a hand grenade. I see something, only to shake my head and see nothing. Finally one of the replacements comes up to relieve me.

Sliding my feet ahead of me through the mud, I manage to work my way back to my hole without falling into anyone's bed.

In the morning there is a break in the weather so Bradford and I climb out and sit on the edge of the slit trench trying to dry out in the momentary sunshine. A herd of white cows is grazing on the hill just below us. While we are watching, an invisible hand snatches up the cows and drops them, scattering them over the grass. As we hear the sound of the explosion one cow struggles to its knees and then falls back dead like the others.

"How senseless it all is," I say to Bradford. "A peaceful herd wiped out just like that. Nothing's safe from artillery."

We hear some yelling and see four medics pulling a man along down the mountain. He is fighting with them and struggling as they hold his arms down.

"Shell shock," Bradford says.

The shelling and screaming meamies continues so we have to duck back into our holes. Day and night we are afraid to get out. To pass time I start reading the copy of "Botany Bay" that I've been carrying inside my shirt. I am escaping, and in my mind I am in colonial Australia.

In the morning we are awakened by the drone of airplanes. Through the broken clouds we can see wave after wave of bombers flying over to blast Bologna. Hour after hour, wave after wave of the flights continue, and from the outpost we can look down on that unfortunate city in the Po valley. It is a major industrial, railroad and supply center and the Krauts are fighting hard to hang onto it.

Again there are the rumors that we are to be relieved---by the Eighty-fifth--by the British. Even the major believes it. It seems that someone will have to relieve us soon since there are so few of us left.

Malik and Davis have disappeared, and I have learned that Sarvo was killed by our own artillery on the same night that Marty died. It seems their destinies were the same. They were rivals all through training, made sergeant at the same time, made staff at the same time, and now died at the same time and in the same way.

Soroyan hasn't been feeling well so he decides to go to the aid station in the church on the hill. When he doesn't come back I think I should go up and see what has happened to him.

The sun has come out and I hope walking to the aid station will dry my wet shirt. It is very quiet as I climb up the path, but the two dead Krauts by the well remind me that it doesn't pay to linger outside.

Although the church is mostly in ruins the front wall is still standing. I am amazed that anything is left after the pounding it has taken. The aid station is in the basement.

Inside the front door there is an entry hall and from there the stairs lead down to the basement. I am ready to start down when I see some men in a room to my right and I think I might as well check in there first. Soroyan may be waiting there.

I am hurled to the floor by a mighty blast! Fine, choking white plaster fills the air and the building is quivering and rocking. Right in front of me the second floor has crashed down, carrying everything into the basement. There is a loud rumble as the brick, plaster and mortar settle. The stairway is gone and ahead of me is open ground and blue sky.

More shells are coming in! leaping up, I race into the room with the other G.I.s. Together we hug the floor and pray silently. Shell after shell thunders in. The church is disintegrating around us. Plaster and fine sand is dropping all over the room.

"The whole basement was buried," a voice says.

"The aid station's buried!"

Hearing this sends a chill through me.

"We need someone to dig a guy out," a voice says.

"Let's help him!" It is Ayer's voice.

"What are you doing here?" I ask with surprise.

"I'm waiting to go to the hospital. I have blood poisoning in my arm." He shows me the red streak between his wrist and his elbow.

I am relieved to see Soroyan lying on the floor too.

Another shell hits the church! The only room left standing is the one we are in. The Krauts are out to level the entire building!

"As soon as the shelling stops for ten seconds I'm going to get out of here and back to my hole," I whisper to Ayers.

There is no answer. The plaster is falling and everyone is lying face down on the floor.

No shells are falling! I begin to count to myself. When I get to ten I jump to my feet and charge out the door. With blind terror I race across the level yard, crash through the brush and head straight down the hill to my hole. Soon Soroyan joins me.

"I swear I'll never go into a building on the front again!" I tell him.

Toward evening the medics take the wounded back down the mountain, and both Ayers and Soroyan go with them.

The shelling on top of the mountain continues, and soon both the church and the house are completely demolished. Most of A Company is wiped out in the house!

After the fifth night the order finally comes to pull back off the mountain. Another battalion is moving in to take over our sector. As our company assembles to start down there are hardly enough of us left to make one good platoon.

What a relief it is to be leaving Mt. Grande. Everything that has happened seems unreal. To add to the feeling that this is a fantasy, we hear someone strumming on a guitar and singing with a southern drawl. One of the new replacements is playing a guitar!

"Where'd you get that?" I ask him.

"Found it in a house," he answers and continues picking and singing.

I look at Martin, the only one left from the original squad. He looks at the relaxed guitar player and shakes his head, smiling.

We have been in action more than fifty days and we're not moving back to the rear. We are just being moved to another part of the front, an area next to Mt. Grande. We also have a new CO., a first lieutenant. We don't know what happened to Lieutenant Mitchel.

It is unbelievable! Our depleted company is not being relieved! And now we have another inexperienced CO. Strangely, I no longer care who is in charge--I don't know any of them. I have developed a fatalistic attitude. I even feel relaxed.

TWENTY-ONE

At last the new C.O. says something, but his manner is that of a stateside officer in garrison. After calling the sergeants and the rest of the company together, he barks out his orders in a dictatorial tone. We have been waiting around like sheep while he stood off by himself studying the valley below through his binoculars. We've been told nothing and have no idea what is going on.

"I'm dividing the company," he says. "One platoon will go down into the valley to set up some outposts. There are some houses there and they have all been cleared. We have tanks down there and you will set up outposts to protect them from German counter attacks.

"The rest of the company will move part way up Mt. Grande and set up another outpost there."

Our platoon is the one chosen to go into the valley. He calls it a platoon, but we have only eleven men, not even a squad.

"The platoon going into the valley," he continues, "will give all their automatic weapons and hand grenades to the men going up Mt. Grande. They may need them."

Then he turns to a new replacement, the medic who has arrived to take Wallace's place. Wallace has finally gone to the hospital with his wounded arm.

"You will go with the platoon in the valley. They are more likely to need you."

"This doesn't make sense," I whisper to Martin. "If we're more likely to need a medic why are we giving up our automatic weapons and hand grenades?"

The CO. finishes his instructions by telling us to take our bed rolls and come back in the morning.

It is near two in the afternoon when our eleven man platoon starts down the slope toward the valley. To our right there is a gulley filled with small trees. We can see a small stream flowing down through it to the valley below. Across the gulley, on a hill above the valley there is a farmhouse.

The stream in the gulley flows into a small river that cuts across the valley in front of the house. That river will be cur first barrier and we'll have to cross it to reach two more houses in the valley.

As we near the river, a man runs out of the house across the gulley and waves his arms in the air. He is not waving to us, but is looking toward the valley. Immediately I am suspicious that it is some kind of a signal.

Several artillery shells explode on the slope behind us! To escape these we slide down into the gulley and continue walking toward the river. We pass by the farmhouse, but only the roof is visible from our low position.

Wading into the river, we find that it is only knee deep. The sergeant leading us, who I don't know, decides we should stay in the water and walk up the river as we advance toward the two houses.

The first house is a low, gray one story building and the ground around it is completely barren. There are no plants or animals to be seen. It looks abandoned, probably cleared by our forces, but not taking any chances, we use the brush and reeds along the river bank for concealment.

Boom! A puff of black smoke hovers in the air near the house.

We crouch down in the water and study the smoke. What is it? Someone says it's a mine, but Martin and I think it is an air burst shell.

Boom! Boom! Two more blasts go off above the river. They are definitely aimed at us.

"They're air bursts," the sergeant says. "If we get into the house it'll give us some protection."

He and the next two men climb out of the river and up the bank. No sooner are they out of the water than a machine gun opens fire. The bullets are spraying the river, churning up the water.

In a surprise move the sergeant and the two men with him dive into the water and race across to the other bank. The gun is firing from the house behind us! The one by the gulley!

The sergeant motions for me to come over, and when the firing stops, possibly so the gunner can change the barrel, I dash across to join him under the bank.

The rest of the men are crouched low in the water across from us. The gun is spraying the river again, but evidently the angle of fire is too high to hit anyone.

The others have got to get across and under the bank before the Krauts move their gun. We keep motioning to them and one by one they make the move. Everytime one crosses, the gun kicks the water again. It is a miracle that they all make it.

However, we are three men short! We haven't seen anyone get hit, but three men are missing and none of us know where they are. We can't see them.

The new medic is missing and so are Barker and Jenkens, who have been with the company for a while. We keep calling them, but there is no answer.

We can't go back without them, so we wait. Everyone is nervous. The Krauts know where we are and they may move the gun. They could even close in on us and start throwing hand grenades.

Finally the sergeant decides we should pull back into the gulley and wait there. Moving is far better than waiting! We creep along under the river bank and then follow the stream about ten yards up the gulley. The Krauts in the house can't see us and it makes us feel better to know they don't know where we are.

We stand waiting for a half hour, but there is still no sign of the missing men. The silence is broken by the sound of a tank moving around in the valley.

"We can't wait any longer," the sergeant decides. "We'll have to pull back past that house where the Krauts have their machine gun."

"They know how we came down and they may try to cut us off," Martin says.

"Yeh," the sergeant agrees. "The longer we wait the more dangerous it is to stay here. We'll stay in the stream and crawl up the gulley past the house."

The water in the creek is icy cold and my feet ache as I climb over the rocks. We can see the roof of the house from the gulley, but the tall reeds around the water should hide us.

We crawl on through the water and everything remains quiet. Once past the house we can breathe easier. Then we again hear the loud rumbling of a tank.

Now I see it! It is just across the river coming toward us and the gun is aimed right up the gulley.

"It's a tiger tank," I say with alarm.

"No," someone disagrees. "It's American. The C.O. said we have tanks down there."

"It's one of those we're supposed to outpost," someone else agrees.

"No! No! It's a German tank!" I insist. "Remember my basic training was in the Tank Destroyers. I know it's a tiger. We were drilled in identification."

"Swoosh—boom!" An eighty-eight mm shell lands up the gulley ahead of us. The argument is settled.

By reflex action we drop into the water, but the motion is useless. The gulley is no protection and if we move out onto the slope we'll be like targets in a shooting gallery. It is nothing for a tank gunner to score a direct hit at such close range.

Desperately my brain flashes through every option. We can't stay in the gulley, and the only place to go is up on the slope. The only way back to the company area is up that same slope, and we'll be in clear view all the time. There is nothing we can do! I'm sure we are in his gunsight right now! I expect every second to be my last!

Suddenly a feeling of calm comes over me. I've done every thing I could do to stay alive these many months. It's hopeless. It is fate! There was no chance from the beginning. I think of Marty and how our artillery finished him off. Maybe the dead ones are not the unlucky ones. We go on and on suffering just to meet some terrible end. It's too bad we have to suffer through all this before we're killed. The lucky ones die right off.

When that gunner touches the button it will all be over. My only regret is that I won't get to see my family once more. I'd like to see them all one more time. Home is a wonderful, distant dream.

I am shaken from my thoughts by the action of the sergeant. He is walking up out of the gulley and starting up the slope toward the company area. Immediately I follow him. We all start walking toward our home base, the only place we have to go. We are condemned men, expecting a quick execution.

We are in plain view of the house across the gulley and the tank across the river. I feel physically exhausted, weak from diarhea and tired from lack of food and sleep. My legs ache again.

It is a slow, slippery climb. On and on up the slope we go in silence. Why doesn't the tank fire anymore? It just sits there with its gun aimed at us. Our steady climbing takes us all the way back while the mighty Tiger remains silent.

When we reach our area we find a few men are dug in around the CO. He is standing in a slit trench with his elbows resting on the ground. The binoculars are still in his hands. He has been watching us.

"What did you find out?" he asks in a matter of fact tone.

I feel the hot blood rising in my temples. Did he send us on a patrol without telling us? Why did he have us give up our automatic weapons and hand grenades? Does he know anything about the valley? Is it really supposed to be secured?

We have three men missing. Doesn't he notice this, or is he unconcerned?

Suddenly I am angry with the whole system of sending replacements to the front piecemeal. None of us know each other or know who we can depend on. My morale is sinking fast.

After eating a K ration I feel worse than ever. My feet and legs ache and I feel very weak. Finally, I tell the sergeant that I think I should go to the aid station and be checked.

He pleads with me to wait until morning. He is afraid the Krauts will counter attack during the night and there are very few of us to defend each other.

I look around at my few buddies and agree to wait. We scatter ourselves along a line in front of a dirty two story farmhouse and dig slit trenches. Martin and I team up.

As soon as it is dark the rain begins comming down in torrents. We have a shelter half stretched over our hole, but it keeps very little water out. Hour after hour Martin and I sit wide awake in the cold water. Our hole gets so full that the water reaches our necks as we sit together with our knees up under our chins.

We can't get out because the tank has started firing. Each shell sounds low enough to take our heads off as it skims over our ridge and slams into the slope above us.

Some of the shells are hitting off to our right and the constant shelling is setting off mud slides and avalanches. We can hear the rumbling masses of dirt and rock hurtling down the slopes causing the mountain to tremble and shake. Our hole is beginning to crumble and cave in, and our greatest fear is that we will be buried by an avalanche from above.

At times my mind is barely conscious of the rocking blasts, for it is numbed by the icy water that totally covers my body. • Martin and I are in an animal state, barely aware of our physical misery. The night is a thousand hours long.

I hear a cry! Martin hears it too. I look at the luminous dial of my watch and it says eleven-thirty. Someone is lumbering up the mountain.

Is it an enemy? We look out into the black rain and listen. Someone is definitely coming up the slope.

"Hey! Company C!" a voice calls out.

"It's them!" Martin says, leaping out of the hole.

When we call to them, Jenkens and Barker drag themselves over to our trench.

"We're both shot in the legs," Barker says. "The machine gun got us. The medic's dead."

"His first day at the front!" Martin says.

"We were all three hit in the legs," Jenkens says. "We laid low in the river, but the medic raised up and was hit again. Barker and I waited until dark before we moved."

What can we say? I can imagine them laying wounded in the river until dark, and then making that long climb up the mountain with painful leg wounds.

"I'm exhausted," Barker says, sitting down on the edge of the hole.

"We'll help you to the house," Martin tells them.

I put my arm around Jenken's waist and Martin helps Barker. Together we shuffle the final hundred yards to the farmhouse. Leaving them with a medic, we return to the icy water of our hole.

Just before dawn there is mere shelling that sends mud and rock cascading into our hole. At that time both Martin and I are injured. His foot is hurt and I have a damaged wrist. In the morning light I can see that my arm is badly swollen.

"I'm going to the aid station this time no matter what happens," I tell Martin.

"I'm going too," he says.

My aching, throbbing legs are more painful than my wrist. I'm limping along with stiff muscles and joints and finally reach the farmhouse. There is no one there, so I drop my light pack and ammo to the ground and prepare to walk on to the aid station.

Before starting down the muddy trail, I lean my rifle against the wall of the house. I have a strong feeling I won't be needing it. As I look down at it resting against the Italian farmhouse. I speak my thoughts.

"The medics may just send me back here, but if not, I hope I never have to pick up a rifle again."

Western Union
SAH35 GOVT=WUX Washington DC 8 232P
Mrs P.Clifford
1944 NOV 8 AM 11 58
5021 Gramercy PL LOSA=

Regret to inform you your son private first class Ron Clifford was slightly injured in action twenty seven October in Italy you will be advised as reports of condition are received=

J A Ulio the Adjutant General

TWENTY-TWO

The aid station is not a long way off. They are never far from the line. It is my aching feet, the constant drizzle and the damn slippery path that creates the illusion of distance.

At last I see it through the mist, a dirty farm building huddled against the mountain. The gray walls are streaked by years of bad weather and it looks too decrepit to be a medical facility. My mind is conditioned to expect more.

Inside, seeing the medic with his white arm band with its red cross calms my doubts. The medic is snuffing out the candles and pulling back the blanket from over the window. This lets in light, but no sunshine. Outside the drizzle has turned to rain and the sky is slate gray.

"Unless you're an emergency you'll have to wait in the shed out in back until you can see the doctor," he tells me. "Give me your name and I'll call you when it's your turn."

In the shed, under the thatched roof, over a dozen men are lying in the hay. Some are sick and others wounded. The waiting doesn't bother me. At least it is dry in here and my injured wrist is more numb than painful.

My first impression on seeing the doctor is that he is amazingly neat. I haven't seen anyone in a clean uniform for a long time. He examines my wrist in a professional manner for several minutes. Then he fastens a tag to my shirt and makes a sling for my arm.

"You should go to the hospital and have this x-rayed. A bone could be broken or it could be a bad contusion."

I am sent back to the shed to wait until a group can be assembled to go to the hospital. A few men have just arrived back from the hospital and they are reporting back to duty. Among them is Denny. He is glad to see me, but doesn't have time to talk.

I hate to see Denny going back into all the mess and confusion, but I know he is desperately needed. Just seeing him back will raise morale in the company--if there is anyone left who knows him.

It is almost noon when a medic comes in to tell eight of us that he will lead us down the trail to a road in the pass. We start out in the rain, slipping and sliding down the clay path. Mud and rocks are washing down the slopes around us as the rain erodes the mountains creating new channels and mud slides.

When we get down the mountain things don't look much better. The road shares the pass with a raging river that is eating away its banks. Although the road parallels the river, it occasionally crosses from one side to another, and all the bridges are down, either blasted by the retreating enemy or swept away by the storm.

To reach the road we have to go across the river and the engineers have strung a metal cable from one bank to the other. They tell us we will have to wade through the swift water hanging onto the cable. The rampaging water is chest high and the footing is difficult.

With one arm in a sling, I know I can never stand up against that raging force. I will have to follow the river and try to find some other way across. I am joined by another injured G.I. who has been wounded in the shoulder.

The river is far above its normal banks, so we have to climb up the slippery slope of the mountain and work our way along above the white water. We finally come to the ruins of a bridge where brick and rock are scattered across the river. By climbing and leaping from one pile of rock to another we are able to work our way across.

The ruined bridge has led us to a small village of rock buildings. A G.I. helps to pull us up the bank and directs us to the aid station.

A number of huge tracked vehicles are parked in the village. They are usually used to pull the large artillery pieces known as "long toms," but are now being used to try to get men and supplies through the water and mud.

"Most of the supplies have washed down into the Po valley," the G.I. says. "Now the Krauts will have to eat K rations."

The medics at the aid station pull us over to the fireplace where a roaring fire is warming the room. While we are standing by the heat in our dripping clothes, they bring us hot coffee and food. They even turn on the radio for us so we can hear Axis Sally playing American music—by Fritz and the boys.

She amazes us with a very candid statement, "If the Russians keep coming we'll be sending the trucks down to haul you boys to Berlin."

There are four other injured G.I.s at the aid station, so the medics arrange to have an ambulance take the six of us down the road. They warn us that the bridges are all out. The ambulance can only take us a few miles to the rear and then we'll have to walk over a foot bridge. Another ambulance will pick us up there.

As soon as our ambulance begins to move, we are back in the war. Kraut artillery is landing all over the road.

We reach the foot bridge, and the shells are falling there too. Jumping out of the ambulance, I drop to the ground. The air is filled with smoke and acrid, burning powder. An Italian soldier with a line of pack mules has just crossed the bridge and the animals are bucking and squealing, terrified by the shells. The Italian is in a panic himself, trying to get the animals off the road. He is hanging onto the reins of the lead animal, but it is rearing and dancing all over.

Leaping up, I race across the wooden bridge toward a house on the other side. An ambulance is in the shadow of the house and as the driver sees us he begins to move the vehicle forward, creeping cautiously. He waves and yells for us to hurry, and we are barely inside the ambulance when the driver spins it around and races down the road to escape the shells.

We only go a short ways before we again come to a ruined bridge. This one is sunk down into the water but is passable by foot. Leaving the ambulance, we scramble, slip and jump across the wreckage. There is nothing on the other side so we set out walking down the road.

We walk for several miles without seeing anyone, but finally when it is dark, we come to a large farmhouse that looks empty and deserted.

Cautiously I slip up to the door, and inside see a large room where a corporal is sitting at a table writing by the light of two burning candles.

Interrupting him, I ask, "Is this some kind of a headquarters?"

"This is the Ninety-first division truck headquarters," he says, looking up.

I ask him if they have an ambulance that can take us to the hospital, but he can't understand how we got here and keeps asking more questions.

Finally, he tells us that he can't supply an ambulance because the motor pool has been washed away by the flood.

"The jeeps rolled over and over, and even the heavy trucks were lost."

Another corporal comes into the room and they get into a discussion about us. No one seems to know what to do, but they want to help us. The corporal who just came in goes back into another room and we hear him trying to contact someone on a phone.

We are all so tired we sit down on the floor. It feels so good to sit down that nothing else matters for the moment. We are in a kind of stupor, and I feel patient and relaxed. We are in a building out of the rain and we hear no sounds of war.

After about a half hour a G.I. comes in and tells us he is a truck driver and he will take us to a hospital. The truck is a small, open ammunition truck and it is difficult for six of us to crowd into the small bed. We don't mind being cramped because the night is freezing and it keeps us warmer to be huddled together.

The night is black and the driver can't use any headlights, but it doesn't seem to bother him. We are bouncing along at a fast clip while the driver talks all the time. He is being cheerful, trying to pep us up.

In the dark night the hospital receiving station looks like a row of volcanos. These pyramidal tents glow like lanterns and they are surrounded by a sea of mud that has been created by the ambulances that are constantly coming and going.

Inside there is a bedlam with people milling around. It is so crowded that we can hardly get inside the door. Wounded soldiers and civilians are standing or sitting on the dirt floor all around the inside of the tent, while in the center, under hanging light bulbs, the doctors are performing emergency surgery.

It is difficult to push past a group of Italian men and women who are hanging on each other sobbing, patting and comforting one another.

"They are all from one family," a G.I. next to us explains. "One of the children stepped on a mine and an older brother rushed over to help and he hit a mine also. It was a mine field. They were trying to rescue each other and they set off five mines altogether."

The doctors are treating soldiers and civilians alike. It is a nightmare, a scene from a horror movie. The light from the naked bulbs casts shadows on the canvas walls. It is a painting from Dante's Inferno.

The truck driver has found the receiving officer, and the first words we hear are that they can't take care of us.

"This is a Ninety-first division hospital and you're from the Eighty-eighth. We're swamped with wounded of our own. You'll have to take them to one of the other places."

The driver spins around on his heel, "We'll see about this!"

He tells us to wait for him in the truck and he disappears around the tent. We follow his instructions.

"Over here!" a voice calls out.

The driver has returned and is walking beside an ambulance guiding it as it slowly backs toward us.

"He'll take you," he tells us.

Gratefully we change vehicles.

The ambulance has only gone a mile when the road divides into three branches. Our driver admits he is lost and decides to park by the road and wait for some vehicle to come along. A large truck creeps slowly past, feeling its way along in the dark. Our driver starts up and follows it.

We are stopped by a British soldier standing in the road waving his hands. He tells us the bridge is out and the British engineers are repairing it. They'll have it finished by morning. There is nothing to do but spend the rest of the night waiting in the ambulance.

Early in the morning we get the signal that the road is open and the ambulance rolls again. The driver takes us to a motor pool instead of a hospital.

"All the hospitals near the front are full, so I'm going to get a truck driver to take you to a hospital back in Florence."

I have become completely passive and am just letting things happen. Anyplace away from the front sounds inviting, and Florence is far to the rear.

We are transferred to a small truck with a canvas cover over the back. The rear is open, giving us our only view of the passing landscape. The massive mountains are rapidly left behind, and along the road the engineers are shoveling the rock and mud away, trying to extricate trucks and heavy guns that are partially buried under the slides.

The sky is clearing and the morning sun gives the foothills and mountains a fresh sharp look, but I know too much of what is happening up there to enjoy the view. They are dark walls hiding terrible secrets. I wonder how long it will be before they find Marty's body in the buried aid station on Mt. Grande. With all the rain and mud slides many G.I.s and Krauts will never be found. Too many went into the Gothic line and didn't come out!

I am amazed that the driver knows exactly where to take us. The truck winds through the streets of Florence and stops in front of a large Catholic hospital.

A medic comes to meet us and leads us up the stone steps, down a wide hall, and into what appears to be a grand council room.

From behind a highly polished table a group of officers, dressed in clean, neatly pressed khaki uniforms, look up as we enter. One of them looks at me and calls for me to step forward. As I stand in front of the table he frowns and stares at me with cold eyes.

"Don't you believe in saluting an officer, soldier?" he snaps sharply.

"Yes, sir," I answer grimly, saluting.

"Why are you so dirty?"He frowns with disgust.

"I was brought here directly from the front. The evacuation hospitals are all filled."

"Why is your arm in a sling?" he asks.

"Because my wrist is injured."

"Who put the sling on it? Did you do it?"

"The doctor at the aid station at the front. He put it on and tied this tag on my shirt."

The officer turns his head and talks with the man next to him. He then assigns me a ward number.

I follow the medic down the hall to the ward, but I am burning with anger. I think of what everyone is going through at the front and wish I had the power to stick this officer up there so he can get an education.

The attitude in the ward is completely different. An army nurse greets me with a big smile and tells me where I can get some water to wash up.

Taking off my helmet, I sink to the bed.

"You wouldn't like to donate that helmet to the hospital would you?" the nurse asks. "We're very short of wash basins and those helmets are perfect."

"Take it," I tell her.

"Thanks," she smiles. "Here, I'll fill it with hot water for you."

When she returns with the helmet I wash the mud from my face, hands and neck and take off the muddy uniform and shoes. Stretching out on the bed, I am instantly in a deep sleep, aware of nothing.

TWENTY-THREE

It is a dream! The smiling face of an American girl is bending over me. Her hair is neatly combed and her voice is soft.

"Wake up. It's time to eat," the army nurse is shaking me gently.

Reality is pouring in from all sides, arousing my consciousness. I fight it. I don't want to leave the womb of my sleep, but it's too late. I remember it all. I'm in the hospital.

"You need to eat," the nurse repeats.

"Is it time for dinner already?" I ask.

"Not dinner, lunch! You slept through dinner and breakfast."

"You mean I slept all night? How long have I been asleep?"

"At least eighteen hours, but that's alright. We just let you sleep. It seems sleep is what you needed most, but now I think you'd better have some food. Also, the doctor wants to examine you."

The doctor examines my wrist and orders x-rays. These show the wrist isn't broken, but there is a bad contusion. He is more interested in my feet than my wrist and wants to know if my legs and feet have been bothering me. When I tell him they've been aching he is not surprised.

"Have you ever heard of trench foot?" he asks.

"No," I tell him.

"Well, you have it. What happens is the circulation in your feet breaks down due to exposure to the wet and cold. It's not like frost bite where the tissue freezes. With trench foot the blood is not circulationg well in the feet. It can be very dangerous--in extreme cases we've had to amputate the affected parts. That is when gangrene sets in. Yours does not appear to be that serious, but we need to take care of your feet and not let things get worse. I want you to stay off your feet completely. You'll have your meals in bed and the only time you'll walk is to go to the latrine. I'm going to prescribe three weeks of bed rest."

I am moved to a large room with many beds in it. It is like being in the lobby of a bank. The ceiling is very high and the floors are of marble. The army nurses look after us, but the Catholic sisters in their black gowns move silently among the beds doing helpful little things.

It has been a long time since I have written to my family and I know the long silence must worry them. Writing letters is my first objective.

Dear Mother, Dad, Gladys, Betty,

This is the first time I've had to write in a long time. I have a sprained left wrist and am in the hospital for a little while. My feet are bothering me a bit--swollen, so I've been ordered to stay in bed. After being up front for so long this isn't hard to do. I feel like a physical and nervous wreck. The sleep I got in the hospital was my first in eighty some hours.

I'm writing this letter with a pen left by a German prisoner at the front.

Your letters have been coming right along and they almost bring tears to my eyes when I read them—they sound so much like you all. You are thoughtful.

I met the corporal who is the chaplain's assistant here, and he is the same one I met in the hospital last summer--the one who wrote to you. We are going to have a talk when I am allowed up.

I hope you'll forgive the awful writing, but I'm not used to writing in bed. This hospital has real beds, the first I've slept in since we left the states. Also we're sleeping between real sheets. It's wonderful!

It's almost Halloween, but there's not a sign of the traditional orange and black. I'm thinking of the celebrations we used to have with pop corn, nuts and cider. Also I remember the box you sent me last Halloween, Betty. Remembering is a pleasant way to pass the time.

Last night I dreamed I came home. I pray for that day constantly. The dream seemed almost real. I dreamed you met me, Betty.

Take care of yourselves—I'll be seeing you,

Love,
Ron

Change is swift and certain in the army. They need the hospital beds for more casualties coming from the front, so those of us who will require beds for several weeks are being moved farther back.

The new hospital is a simple army hospital set up in pyramidal tents, but it is near Leghorn and any movement away from the front raises my morale.

Winter is coming and we are chilled by the strong winds that sweep down from the snow crowned mountains. Our beds are army cots and we try to stay under the wool blankets to keep warm.

I only get up to walk to the Latrine which is in another tent about twenty yards away. There is a wooden walk that leads to it and the biting wind squirms up under my bathrobe every time I go out.

The doctor is a captain in his mid thirties and he rarely talks as he examines me, but seems very methodical and efficient. He questions me a great deal about my condition and writes down all the information in a folder.

There are only a few patients in the large ward, so it is quiet and lonely. There is no music or public address system. I feel isolated and am not use to such privacy, but compared to the front it is heaven. I pass the time by reading and writing letters.

One uneventful day follows another. For two weeks I rest, but I wonder what the future has in store for me. I wonder if my division is up in those mountains covered with snow. Will I be going back soon? I don't want to think about it.

It is the beginning of the third week and the doctor comes in late in the afternoon. As usual he looks at my feet carefully. This time he says much more.

"With your feet you can't go back up there in this winter weather. You won't be ready for duty until spring, and by then the war will be over.

"I'm going to send you south to Naples for the winter. It's warmer down there and that will be better for your feet."

The doctor is smiling as he speaks. He is saving my life and he knows it. Our eyes meet and what is it that I see? Compassion? A friend?

"Thank you, sir," is all I can say.

I feel like an invalid. The medics insist on carrying me on a litter. I am not allowed to walk to the ambulance and I don't want things this way.

"Doctor's orders," they tell me.

The ambulance takes me through the streets of Leghorn to the waiting hospital ship. As we bounce along over the cobblestones I can look through the back window and see many holes in the road where the engineers have been digging up mines.

Again the medics carry me—up the gangplank and into a ward on the ship. It is a large room with dozens of hospital beds and I am assigned one by the window.

We sail early in the morning and it is a clear, sunny day. There is a pleasant, feminine voice that gives instructions to us on the public address system. There is also music from several speakers in the ward,

"I'll be seeing you, in all the old familiar places"

The hospital ship, Hynd, stays close to the coast. The green and brown hills and bluffs of the coast slip slowly past the window. What a change in the weather! Only a few cotton clouds drift across a deep blue sky.

Suddenly the ship stops! For an hour we are dead in the water. When the explanation comes over the P.A. system it is a grim reminder that our peaceful enclave is still surrounded by outside threats and things can change very quickly.

"A floating mine almost hit the ship, but it is safe to proceed now."

I look around at the casualties in the beds and have terrible visions of what might have happened. Many men are badly mutilated and helpless. One, two beds away from me, has no arms and no legs. I look at that trunk with a head and think I would rather not go back at all. But what choice does he have? How could he commit suicide?

The ship is filled with brave men!

We sail across Naple's huge harbor and it looks the same as when I first arrived from Africa. The same wrecked ships are in the harbor and bomb blasted wharfs are unrepaired.

However, this time I ride from the docks instead of walking, as before. The streets are filled with people, the usual begging children and the men and women with their brightly painted carts being pulled along by white oxen or horses. The ambulance can barely move through the congestion.

The hospital is at the fairgrounds where the international exposition would have been held had the war not forced Mussolini to change his plans. Many of the modern buildings have been made into wards, but the trench foot cases are in a long tent.

I am surprised at the great number of trench foot cases inside. The cots are so close together they almost touch each other, two rows of them with an aisle down the center. There must be thirty cots in each line. One of these is to be my new home.

Two days after my arrival I begin to feel nauseated and during the night I go down to the latrine at the end of the tent and throw up. I mention this to the G.I. in the next bed and he tells the nurse. She is angry with me for not having told her, but I explain that it is nothing.

In the afternoon the doctor comes in to examine me and he pulls down my eyelids to see the color of my eyes. He thinks the whites look a little yellow, and he orders a blood test. The medic who is with him is all prepared and immediately draws a tube of blood from my arm.

Again I am moved. This time I am taken from the tent and placed in a room in a building. There are six other patients and we all have hepatitus.

Since my address is changed again, I have a lot of letters to write. Also, my mail is catching up with me at last. Some letters were written many weeks ago.

October 10, 1944

Dear Son,

Betty is sitting here writing to Charles as usual. She hasn't heard from him for several days and that worries her.

Dad bowled for the Legion last night, but said he was off his form and didn't do very well. Of course, never having bowled myself, I know nothing about it.

Kitty was in meeowing his head off, so I gave him some milk and he's gone again. Gladys wants to get a dog, but I told her it's so hard to get meat I think she had better wait until after the war.

I haven't felt well for several days. It seems everyone is having the flu. The neighbors have all had it and Dad says everyone at work has been sick.

Last night I painted two little tables green and today I painted the beach umbrella, but it will have to have another coat. We can use them in the yard. Betty and Gladys are both working so I'm alone more now.

I talked with Jim's mother and she said he is overseas in the Pacific. Barry is over there too. You know how his mother always worries about him. Everyone is certainly worried now.

Ellen, across the street, married someone in the air corps. It seems everyone is getting married.

I think Betty is going to send you the sports news.

Well, I've told you everything I can think of this time. I'll write again tomorrow.

Take care of yourself and if you want anything just write for it.

With Lots of Love,

Mother

October 24,1944

Dear Ron,

Well how's the kid? This place is deader than a door nail so there's not much to write about. Mother and I are going shopping tomorrow. I'm going to get some shoes and a hat--that is if I can find anything decent. I've decided to make a dress for Mother because that's what she needs.

I've already decided to call the little dog we're going to get Butch--don't you think that's cute. Dad is very much against the idea of getting a dog. I think he's afraid his prized victory garden will be uprooted".

I'm going to an exercise class at the YWCA with the girls at work. I weigh 120 pounds—that's the most I've ever weighed.

I had the girls from Firestone over last night. They're all so nice. We fixed some enchaladas. They didn't look like the picture but they were good. I'll fix you some when you get home. The corn meal pancakes are supposed to be rolled up but ours wouldn't roll—so we just put one pancake down flat and put the chili mixture over that and put the other pancake on top like a sandwich. I loved it and everyone else seemed to like it too.

I thought up a new cocktail to serve them too—it's my version of a mint julip. I got some mint flavoring, some green food coloring, some whisky and ginger ale. Doesn't that sound good? Everyone said they liked it. Then we played with the ouija board.

I got two rolls of film! A girl at work gave them to me. Her boyfriend brought them in but they didn't fit her camera.

We went to the show and saw "In Our Time" with Ida Lupino, and they showed a cartoon. It was one with that cute little rabbit. They have all these ridiculous war pictures now. I don't see why they don't wise up and realize nobody wants to see them.

Betty and I enrolled in an art class--it's 7:00 to 9:30 every Wednesday. They had a model and we had to do fifteen minute sketches from different poses. Boy, am I terrible. I hope I can learn something. It's the only art class they have at the high school.

Well, I've 'got to go. Take care of your little self and I'll see you soon.

Lots of Love,

Gladys

P.S. I'll enclose some of my drawings as soon as they're good enough.

November 17, 1944

Dear Ron,

Guess who!! I can just see you now naming off a couple of dozen girls' names. You can stop. This is your big sister. Well, anyway your sister. I don't exactly like the sound of that big in there.

I can't remember what I told you the last time I wrote. Oh well, you probably hear the same stuff a couple of dozen times anyway by the time everyone writes to you. I can just see you sitting in bed with this in your mit. Gee, I'd like to be sitting on the bed talking to you.

The boss gave a party for the employees Saturday night and I went with a couple of the girls. We had more fun. We got the whole office thoroughly gossipped over, and we played the roulette wheel for a while. Everyone got so many chips and it wasn't too long before everyone had lost every one. We also had a couple of drinks. Yes, just a couple. You should see where the man lives. He lives down in Manhatten Beach and the fog was so thick you could cut it with a knife. It's a wonder we didn't end up in the ocean.

I told Dad that now that I'm home I think it is a good time for me to learn to drive. He just quietly glared at me. I don't know if it is the gas rationing or just my technic. Anyway, something tells me I'm going to wait for Charles to come home. He's the one who appreciates me.

I received two letters from Charles Friday. You mentioned that you never hear from him. It's funny because he said he heard from you and he writes to you. You'll probably get them two years from now.

Gladys, a girl friend and I went to the show last week and saw "Without Love" with Katherine Hepburn. It was good. She's a good actress.

I've been working ten hour days, but had the week ends off to loaf. Now I have to work until 12:30 on Saturdays, so my nose is back at the grindstone. But I don't mind--just look what the soldiers work.

It looks like Germany will soon fold up. I sure hope so. Maybe you will get a discharge then. It would be wonderful to have you home again to stay. It sounds like a wonderful dream. I hope they don't send Charles to the Pacific. I'd much rather he'd stay with the occupation troops. Darn these wars anyway! I'm a lonesome cookie.

Well Myron, it is getting late and I must get up early— darn it. So long for now and take care of yourself.

Love,
Betty

November 27, 19 44

Dear Mother, Dad, Gladys, Betty,

If you will notice, my address is changed again. Besides trench foot I now have yellow jaundice. This is caused by the liver not functioning right, and may be caused by diet.

At present we have skim milk three times a day, in between meals and with meals. We have all the broiled steak we can eat. It seems the more steak we eat the better.

Quite a few people over here get yellow jaundice. So I guess it's just one of those things that goes with the times. The chaplain's assistant had it last year.

By staying on this diet you get over it o.k. and it isn't serious. It's nothing for you to worry about.

I was weighed the other day and only weighed 134 stripped. I weighed 137 when I came into the army. I guess living on all those rations did most of this to me, but I look healthy—to me, and I felt healthy until a couple of days ago. Now that I've been on this diet I feel better. They'll probably fatten me up with this milk. I knew I should have my milk!

I've got a bunch of pocket edition books I'm going to start reading. Most of them are mystery stories.

I sent you some Italian Christmas cards—personally I like American ones better.

We have music here now and that is good. How is your record collection coming? I read where Victor is recording again, and I think Bluebird is too.

Have you heard from Charles? The front in France seems to be active. I'll bet he washes he were back in the air corps. They really treat you well in the hospital.

Take it easy and be careful.
With my Love,
Ron

December 1, 19 44

Dear Son,

Received two letters yesterday and one today, which makes me very happy. Hope you are getting a good rest in the hospital. Maybe if you will be unable to stand the cold weather they'll put you somewhere else. Or is that too much to hope for?

We've started to do our Christmas shopping at last. I have all of Betty's presents. She's been wanting something to wear so I bought her a lovely blouse and a flannel night gown. I bought her another blouse for Dad to give her, and I got her the prettiest blue sweater as your gift for her. Gladys saw it in the window of Robinsons and liked it so well. That is all I have so far.

I think you should have received some of your packages before now. You know I sent you another five pounds of candy only a week later than the other one. In fact we have sent you so many I have lost track of them myself. And it's just going to be too bad for somebody if you don't get them.

Betty is writing to Charles and Gladys is going to put in a note.

I like the poem you wrote for the soldier's wife. It sounds sweet. I bet he appreciated it. You spoke of being cold. I take it they have no heat in the hospital.

Dad went bowling last night but didn't do very well. He is working tonight until midnight.

We have been having quite nice weather for a while, but it looks like rain tonight. I heard over the radio that they had a very heavy snow there in Italy, where you were. It must be very cold there now. Some of the mothers of your friends called and want me to call if I know anything more about you.

Well, this is about all I can think of until tomorrow. Take good care of yourself and if you want anything ask.

With Lots of Love,
Mother

Every day the medics take more blood samples to keep track of my progress. My arms are riddled with needle marks like I'm addicted to something.

There have been some deaths in the hospital from hepatitus, but everyone in our ward seems to be getting better. We have a wonderful nurse we call "Mom." She is like a mother hen with her brood, checking to see that we wash behind our ears and telling us when we need haircuts.

An Italian barber comes in to shave us and cut our hair. Sometimes he brings a little girl with him. She is scrubbed pink and neatly dressed—very cute and obviously his pride and joy. This is one of the few things to break the monotony as one day leads into the next.

Most of the time I read or write my letters. The mail is coming regularly so I don't feel as far away from my family and friends as before. They tell me of new songs and movies. I haven't seen a movie since early August, but I hardly miss them. When on the line there was no time to think about it and when off the front I'm too satisfied to care.

We are thinking and talking about Christmas in the ward, and I'd like to send some souveniers to my family and friends, but there's no chance of getting out. I'm not permitted to walk around anyhow.

When I ask Mom if there is any way to buy anything, she tells me that she sometimes gets a pass and if I'll give her the money she'll get something for my parents.

We can tell the season of the year by the mail. Everyone is receiving boxes of cookies and candy. The doctors have forbidden us to eat any sweets. In fact, we can't eat anything that is not on our strict diet, so the boxes are accumulating under the beds.

December 7, 19 44

Dear Mother, Dad, Gladys, Betty,

Well, three years ago the U.S. went to war. Who would have thought we'd be starting our fourth year of war with peace still a long ways off? It can't last forever—or can it?

The nurse went to town yesterday and I gave her the money to buy a little statue. The one she got is really nice. It is a miniature of a larger statue and is white ceramic. There is a mark on the bottom that means it is real good stuff. It looks like a little beggar--a vagabond singer. I hope you get it all in one piece.

The nurse helped me wrap it. We put it in a coffee can you sent full of cookies. We lined it with army papers and she got me some cotton.

I was reading that a barber threw a Hawaiian born Japanese, who is in the Fifth Army, out of his barber shop. The Japanese fellow wears a purple heart and walks with a crutch. It burns me up to think people are so narrow minded. We worked with the Japanese over here and they are good fighters. I've seen them in the hospital too. They're very American.

It's funny how much more worked up the people back there get than the front line soldiers. I believe the soldiers at the front are the most liberal minded toward the enemy. They sort of realize their predicament and that they suffer and are as human as we are.

We made some Christmas decorations yesterday out of candy and ribbon. These are to decorate the hospital--to get into the Christmas spirit. I'll bet you're getting your decorations out at home too. It's about time to start playing the record White Christmas. Gladys, or Betty, maybe you could paint me a little picture of the Christmas tree.

Well, be careful—I'll be seeing you.
With my Love,
Ron

P.S. I was glad to hear that the schools published the book of war poems and included the one I wrote.

December 21, 1944

Dear Mother, Dad, Gladys, Betty,

The doctor said I'm over the jaundice so I'm back in the trench foot ward. Now I can eat anything I want to. And I got paid for the first time in three months, with was a good thing since I only had three dollars left.

Three more packages arrived, and have I accumulated the food! Everyone is getting so many packages that the fellows smile and say "no thanks" when you offer them anything to eat. How I love to eat! There'll be plenty of food this Christmas, thanks to you all. Your can of home made candy came today, Gladys. There's just nothing like it--out of this world, strictly!1 There was a box of banana flakes, pineapple juice and cookies. I haven't tasted bananas in months.

Then came the surprise box with the wallet—just what I needed. Mine was ruined by all the water at the front. The knife was another thing. I've been having to open packages with a razor blade. The local signorinas would love the perfumed soap. The sweater and socks will help keep me warm.

Everything was wrapped so beautifully—it's just like it used to be. You're the ones who make Christmas and you've brought a fine one to me over here. In all this war and hate, it's like another world. You all prove that kindness still exists. I never realized what a rare family I have until I was on my own in this army. God bless you all. I don't think any family thinks more of each other than we do.

There was a little boy here today that is an orphan. An American sailor off of a liberty ship sort of adopted him. He is about twelve and was all dressed up neatly in a navy uniform. He's been with the ship about a year now and can speak good English. He's very well mannered and when the G.I.s offer him anything he always tells them they should keep it for themselves, but of course they never do.

I haven't heard from Charles. I hope he never gets into action.

You've all made me very happy. I'll have sweet dreams about it all.

Be careful—I'll see you soon.

With my Love,
Ron

December 23, 1944

Dear Mother, Dad, Gladys, Betty,

Tomorrow is Christmas Eve and I'm glad you're all safe at home and can have a peaceful Christmas.

There's a little Italian boy here, fourteen years old, who comes around every day to talk and run errands for the G.I.s. He speaks fairly good English now. He has one foot off at the ankle and both his parents were killed in an air raid. He's been running errands for us for several months and uses the money he makes to pay for his only sister's room and board at school.

His sister has been sick for several weeks and the G.I.s have been giving him things to take to her. She's twelve.

Yesterday his sister died. He came in this morning and broke down and cried and cried. I felt like crying too.

I gave him a bar of the soap you wrapped so pretty. He was pleased, but didn't want to unwrap it. He said it would be nice to just sit it on the dresser and look at it. So, I had one already unwrapped that I gave him to use. I also fixed up a box with some of the brownies you sent, a couple of candy bars, two packs of cigarettes that he can sell, and some cookies. I'm going to give this to him tomorrow. I feel so sorry for him. In war it's the innocent who often suffer.

An Italian man named Angelo comes in and plays the accordian He was on the Italian radio before the war and he is very good. When he played Ave Maria today it sounded so peaceful--really caught the Christmas spirit.

I'm always thinking of you and praying to be with you again soon. Take care of yourselves--I'll be seeing you soon.

With my Love,
Ron

P.S. We are all very upset by the war news on the western front. It is very discouraging.

December 24, 1944

Dear Mother, Dad, Gladys, Betty,

I got a bunch of letters from you all today, the latest one written December 12. They made another Christmas present.

Thanks for the large maps Mother. They really show the way things stand. I believe Charles is in the Ninth Army.

Last night I was talking with an Italian soldier who works here at the hospital. He was a tank driver in Africa when Italy was still in the war. We talked about the world situation, campaigns, etc. His home is in Pompeii and he's going home over Christmas, so I gave him some candy to take to his little boy.

Like all Italians I've met he hates the British more than anyone else and likes the Russians and Americans. A lot of the Italian soldiers fought in Spain.

I'll write again tomorrow.

Be careful--I pray I'll see you soon.

With my Love,
Ron

December 25, 1944

Dear Mother, Dad, Gladys, Betty,

Today we've really been treated royally. First, we woke up and found a big red stocking tied to the foot of the bed. It was filled with fruit, nuts, candy and a pair of socks.

Then the Red Cross came around and gave everyone a box of candy, gum, cigarettes, some little books, a mirror and a folder for pictures. The head nurse came in with some egg nog she had fixed, and we each had a glass. It was sure good--positively delicious!

This afternoon a group of Waacs came in all smiles and joy and spent the rest of the day with us. They were loaded down with presents they had fixed. They gave me a jar of mixed nuts, cigarettes, gum, a large can of pineapple and some candy. Wasn't that nice of everyone? To top things off we had a wonderful Christmas dinner--turkey, potatoes, cranberries, olives, pickles, vegetable, sliced pears and minced pie. I'm so full I can hardly move.

It is sure cold here and the wind blows a lot.

I read where the soldiers' candidate for the man of the year award is the man, who through his carelessness caused the fire and destruction of a plant that produces dehydrated potatoes. They heartily recommend that he be given a job at the plant that produces dehydrated eggs.

The Italians celebrate Christmas like we do the Fourth of July, with fire crackers and noise. A lot of racket, but everyone is happy.

There's so much going on I can't concentrate. The Waacs are back.

Every night I pray to see you soon.

With my Love
Ron

Our ward is settling down to a routine after the excitement of Christmas. However, I have one more pleasant surprise. A buddy that I came over seas with, Jim Andrews, is here in the same hospital. I look up from my reading and see him wandering down the aisle in our tent.

"Hey, Andrews," I yell to him. "What are you doing in here?"

"Locking for any buddies I might know?" he answers. "I guess I was looking for you."

"How did you know I was here?"

"I didn't, but figured there might be somebody from the old outfit around here."

"It's funny we'd see each other here in the hospital, because the last time I saw you was when I was going to the aid station near Palaya, last summer. From there I went to the hospital," I tell him.

"That's right," Andrew remembers. "Things were tough then. It's easier to talk here."

"Are you a patient or do you work here now?" I ask him.

"Got a few internal injuries in a shelling," he explains. "I'm getting better. They decided to let me walk around."

"You should have been in here yesterday," I tell him. "We really had a Christmas party--but I suppose you had one in your ward too."

"There was a party everywhere. It was fun. First party I've been to since leaving the states."

"Do you remember the last party at the E.M. center before we went over seas?" I ask him.

"At Fort Meade?"

"Yes---I never saw a room so packed. It was wall to wall G.I.s and the air was blue with smoke," my mind drifts back. "Everyone was standing around drinking beer watching the show. Remember there was a western band with a girl singer."

"The one dressed in a short skirt and wearing a cowboy hat," he adds.

"Right," I continue. "It was getting late and everyone kept yelling for one more song. We all wanted the night to last forever. We knew that after that it was work and war.

"I remember you were there, and Clancy and Pace and there were some Free French soldiers who had been in the states training and were headed back. We didn't know where we were going and they gave me some addresses in France, in case we ended up there.

"That was a sadly happy night, if you know what I mean. We were frantically happy, knowing it was the last party.

"Finally the girl rubbed her forehead with her hand, pushed back her cowboy hat, and said, 'no more! I'm too tired.'"

"But the gang around her wasn't tired," Andrew says. "They kept shouting for more."

"Yes, so the band played on and the leader wanted to do more, but the girl quit and said it was enough. The band leader gave up then and they played 'Til We Meet Again.

Please wait and pray each night for me,

Till we meet again."

"The party was over!" Andrews finishes.

"Yes, the last party for many months and the last one ever for Pace and some of our other buddies." I add.

Andrews doesn't stay long. He's not supposed to be here in the first place, but this doesn't bother him.

"I don't worry about anything anymore," he tells me. "Whatever is supposed to happen to you will happen. You can die in this hospital just as easily as you can die on the front. If it's your time, it's your time."

"Since I've been here I haven't seen anyone die," I disagree. "At the front a lot of my buddies were killed."

"In some wards here people are dying," he says. "You can't change destiny."

Some of the Brazilian troops from the Brazilian Expeditionary Force are moved into the trench foot ward. One of them is in the bed next to me. He doesn't speak English—none of them do. They have a Brazilian nurse to take care of them, but the Italian prisoners who work in the ward serve the meals and do the clean up for them just as they do for the rest of us.

The Brazilian nurse is very aloof. Whenever we speak to her I think she assumes we are being fresh or trying to seduce her. If we say anything at all she gives us a dirty look.

The Italians don't understand the Brazilians as they speak their native Portugese, but the Mexican-American soldiers can talk with them. Since these Americans can also talk to the Italians, they have become the interpreters.

One of the Brazilians has a clarinet which he plays very well. Most of the music is modern American songs, and he plays them all without music.

Today a light snow is falling and the Brazilians are so excited that many of them are running around outside in their bare feet. The nurses are furious, trying to chase them back inside. It is an insane riot since they all have trench foot and are not even supposed to be out of bed.

The snow has made it colder than usual in the ward. We have three wood stoves that are supposed to keep it warm inside, but that is impossible in a big tent. Half of the time the stoves aren't working well anyhow. We call them the three little Vesuviuses because they are usually smoking.

Our ward looks like an Indian encampment with everyone sitting on his cot wrapped in a wool blanket writing, reading or playing cards. I am reading the New Testament, planning to read it all the way through. I don't know why I decided to do this, but I'm finding new meaning and it stimulates my thinking. With this terrible war in Europe I'm wondering how so many people dare to call themselves Christians.

Some of the Brazilians are keeping us entertained continually. One enjoys attention so much that he parades up and down the aisle imitating the nurses and the Italians with exaggerated gestures. He sometimes marches around nude and acts like a burlesque dancer.

Everyday a doctor checks my feet. We have two different doctors and they come around regularly on alternate days. One of the doctors is a captain and the other a major. Yesterday when the major came he told me that I should continue to remain in bed and stay off my feet. He said the only time I am to get out of bed is when I need to use the latrine.

Today the captain is in the ward and I watch him slowly moving down the line checking everyone's feet. A medic, as usual, follows along with him writing down notes on a clip board.

"You have been in the hospital a long time," the captain says, examining my chart. "I think you should report back to duty. Tomorrow you report to the light duty section."

I can't believe what I am hearing and I answer immediately.

"Sir, the major was here yesterday and he told me that I was not to get out of bed except to go to the latrine. He said it was important that I remain in bed. Until the major changes the order I think that's what I should do."

I can see anger in the captain's face. He glares at me and says nothing. He is outranked by the major, but I'm not sure how important that is among the doctors. The captain turns away and goes to the next bed.

I am worried about this unexpected confrontation and I don't believe I've heard the last of it. I expect the captain will discuss it with the major and I don't know what to expect. I'll be anxiously awaiting the major's visit tomorrow so I can explain what happened.

To take my mind off my concern, I turn to my mail. My Dad has not been writing as often lately, but I have recently received a couple of letters from him.

December 31, 1944

Dear Son Myron,

Well, the final days of the old year are rolling by. The family is in the living room listening to the Hour of Charm program. You remember that do you not? I was in there too dozing in the big chair half dreaming and wandering thousands of miles away, mostly with you. I wonder what the coming year will bring--peace or more heart aches and tears to so many homes and boys.

Since you went away I have realized more than ever the many things we could have done together and didn't. I guess mostly because my struggle for that weekly paycheck was so binding and most of the time it was insufficient to meet the need. Now the check has increased so it actually covers our needs and then you can't be with us, but as you requested, I offer many a silent prayer for your immediate and safe return.

As I was half asleep several thoughts went through my mind that I wanted to write to you, but they have escaped me. I am in the wide awake world and so I will try to think of some things to write.

You mentioned in one of your letters that the physical pain was not so bad, and I believe I know a little of what you mean. Pain is one thing that I could usually get mad over and conquer, but the mental thoughts I've had at times were impossible to put aside.

How do you manage in the hospital? It used to drive me nuts and I only had ten days of it at one stretch. Our diatician was a stinking stomach robber.

Everything is fine at home except for the usual winter colds. There is quite an epidemic of flu in L.A. but so far I've escaped it. Guess I'm too tough for the germ.

Sure can sympathise with you on your sore feet because mine have bothered me ever since 1916 and unless I baby them they hurt terribly at times. Are there any rumors about being sent home or are they going to keep you there until the warm weather comes?

The Russians are getting close to Prussia and the home of the old German Junkers. I think the end may be near and hope for an end to this terrible calamity.

Things are quiet here except for an occasional argument from Gladys, but she is a good youngster. I have a fine family.

Well son, will close wishing you a very happy New Year and praying for your homecoming real soon.

Love and Best Wishes,
Dad

January 4, 1945

Dear Dad,

In your recent letter you asked if I was walking around yet. No Dad, this is my second month in the hospital and I'm still a bed patient. Everytime I am on my feet they burn and swell, but in due time they will be better. As you say, they will always be sensitive to the weather, etc.

Also you asked about my buddies. Well, Dad, I've been broken up from different units so much that I've never become close to anyone. I've sort of steered a middle course being nice to everyone (I hope) and trying to take care of myself. However, in combat my main fear was in being alone. I'm not nearly as scared when someone is with me. I guess we help keep each other calm. Then, we figure that two of us are more apt to detect danger than one. However, the men in the outfits are always being replaced and half of the people are strangers all the time.

On one push our squad started out with thirteen men, a few days later there were only four of us left--the rest casualties. Then replacements brought the squad up to eleven, but in a few days there were only three of us left. Then more replacements came, but after a week we had so few left they incorporated us into another squad. So you can see the chances of keeping a permanent buddy.

One fellow I was with most of the time was lucky. We dug our slit trench together all the time. He was dark, and although his name was Ayers, we called him "Arab" --but he was very good natured and generous. One day we had a shell land about two feet from our slit trench and all of our equipment was blown to pieces so we didn't even have a rifle left. He went to the hospital with shell shock. We were both blown out of the hole by the explosion. Later he came back but got infection in his arm and went to the hospital again.

Another fellow was Pollock from Chicago. I guess we were closer than the others. He was in my company in the states and a fellow wireman on maneuvers. Overseas he was hit in the shoulder by shrapnel and was reclassified and is now waiting for reassign-ment. He is the only one I keep up a correspondence with.

I hate to think of the front. A couple of times I had to resign myself to the idea that I would never get out--things were so bad, but God was with me and answered my prayers.

Things are fine here in the ward. We have a lot of Brazilians now, and they are friendly and well mannered.

It is beginning to rain again, and my feet are burning--the dampness I guess.

Be careful now—and I'll be seeing you.

With Love,
Ron

After a night's sleep I am still worried about my disagreement with the captain and I'm trying to think of what to say to the major. I am anxious for him to come around so I can get it over with.

I wait all morning, and it isn't until after lunch that I see the doctor and his aide working their way slowly up the line from bed to bed. When he finally reaches me I speak up immediately.

"The captain was here yesterday to examine us and he told me that I should report to light duty, but I told him that you had examined me the day before and ordered me to stay in bed. You specifically said I was only to get up to go to the latrine. I told the captain that until you changed my orders I thought I should do as you said."

The major listens to me without comment, but it is obvious he is listening to every word. When I am finished he peels back the blanket and studies my feet carefully. He feels them and lifts them.

I lay waiting for some answer and to myself I say a silent prayer asking God not to send me back into action—asking God in Jesus name as the New Testament has instructed me.

The major covers my feet again and turns to the medic beside him, giving some instructions. I can't hear what he is saying.

The medic takes a tag from the clip board and writes "Z.I." on it in heavy black crayon. He is wiring it to my cot.

"What does Z I mean?" I ask him.

"That's Zone of Interior, the states," the medic answers.

"We're sending you home," the major adds---and smiles.

Peace, a word that no one knows,
From each fight the next one grows.
Generations
Hear the song and join the beat
With marching feet.
War is again reborn,
It's endless.

EPILOG

I left Italy as I had arrived, as an individual, unattached to any particular division. Before going I gave away all the things I had accumulated from the PX and the packages from home. The Italians who worked for us and entertained us in the hospital appreciated the cigarettes and food, and the G.I.s could always use more of the good things from the other world.

Angelo, the accordian player, gave me a souvenier letter opener that had a sculptured woman as a handle.

"It has Italy, 1945 engraved on it," he said. "Something to to take with you to remember Italy."

The medics carried me on a litter to the waiting ambulance and carried me again from the ambulance up the gangplank of the hospital ship. It was early evening, and we sailed immediately. The Acadia, as the ship was named, was a fast ship, a converted liner, and by morning we had already sailed past Gibraltar and were in the rough Atlantic.

On board ship the nurses gave us each a postcard picture of the ship and a flyer with information and instructions. It was designed to make us feel welcome, and it had a philosophical beginning:

"You have served your country in a time of need, and although you have been through terrible times you have had those rare experiences that few in life will ever know. Having survived them you will find you would not trade them for a million dollars."

NOTES AND QUOTES

I can hardly believe you're here in the good old U.S.A. I'm telling you your call just laid us in the aisle with excitement. We were half through lunch when the phone rang and we could hardly believe it when they said it was you calling. I tell you I was just weak. None of us could finish our lunch. You can't imagine the relief.

Gladys

.........I'm just hoping and praying you get that discharge. It'll be the happiest day of my life. No, I think the day you got home on leave from overseas was the happiest day of my life. You looked exactly the same. I was so happy I heard bells.

Gladys

.........I'm just waiting to put the army suit in moth balls. A good idea don't you think?

Mother

I'm still here in dear old Italy. I've got 56 points and should be in the states by Feb. Hope you feel O.K. and no ill effects of the war. I'm glad that we made it O.K. I think we were awfully lucky!
Write when you can. I'll be down to see you sometime in '46 Your Pal, Ruff*
*A buddy who went overseas with me but was sent to a different combat division.

FINALE

War Weary

Kill the present with a song,
The survivors are the strong.
To live longer
Learn to play the game,
Always the same
War is the human play
That's endless.

Wine and party every night,
Kill the past and still the fright
Days are destruction,
Death and killing no one wants,
The memory haunts
And the tormenting dreams
Are endless.

Through the rainy night we go
On terrain we do not know
While the lightning
Is bouncing from cloud to cloud
With thunder loud,
A repetitious scene
That's endless.

Far from home while years go by,
With a choice to fight or die.
Try to explain
A story that makes no sense,
It's self defense.
Our only time is now,
It's endless

Through each child we see our past
In a world that didn't last,
When we felt love
And knew what it was to touch,
We miss it much,
Caught in a total war
That's endless.

Peace, a word that no one knows.
From each fight the next one grows.
Generations
Hear the songs and join the beat
With marching feet.
War is reborn,
It's endless.

Identification

Marty Smitty Winfield 0. Smith
Denny Davey Edward J. Davey
Ayers Eyre Leon S. Eyre
Martin Smith
Allen Miller (medic)
Wallace Miller
Capt. Mathews Captain Matney Capt. Cecil A. Matney
Lt. Lyons Lt. Lyons First Lt. Robert I. Lyons
Rule Rudd Louis L. Rudd
Scotty Campbell
Truett Pellerin Jerald Pellerin
Soroyan Pyzbician
Malik Kubla Anthony Kubla
Pace Page Orin L. Page
Davis Steele
Sarvo Sabo Ernest G. Sabo
Clancy Delaney
Pollock Skrundz Alfred V. Skrundz
Lt. James Plante Raymond Plante